THE PEOPLE PLACES AND EVENTS
OF JEFFERSON COUNTY PENNSYLVANIA

Volume 1

Carole A. Briggs

CLOSSON PRESS
257 Delilah Street
Apollo, PA 15613-1933

ISBN 978-0-9714702-3-1

Copyright @ 2016 by the Jefferson County Historical Society, Inc. All rights reserved. Printed in the United States of America. Except for brief quotations used in critical articles or reiews, no part of this publication may be reproduced or transmitted in any form by any means, electronic or mechanical, including photocopying, recording, or any information storage/retrieval system, without written permission of the copyright owner. For information, write to the Jefferson County History Center, PO Box 51, Brookville, Pennsylvania 15825.

CONTENTS

OUR NATIVE AMERICANS AND THE SENECA 1

NO MATTER THE NAME 5

THERE'S NO PLACE LIKE A SHANTY 9

TOOLS FOR TIMBER 13

FARMING WITHOUT JOHN DEERE 17

JEFFERSON COUNTY'S JOHNNY APPLESEED
.... 21

IN THE DEAD OF WINTER 25

GROWING GREEN 29

MISS MARTHA 33

WHY VICTORIAN? 37

HERE COME THE JUDGES 45

WATER, WATER, EVERYWHERE! 51

BROOKVILLE'S GREAT HALLS 55

THE MILLINERS OF BROOKVILLE 59

THE SEAT OF JUSTICE 65

THAT MOST ESSENTIAL COMMODITY 69

BELLY UP TO THE BAR! 75

THE UNDERGROUND RAILROAD IS NOT A
SUBWAY 79

AND WHAT DID YOU SEE, CHARLEY
ANDERSON? 83

THE DEAD WRITERS SOCIETY 87

24/7 SERVICE AT THE PUMP 95

WHAT'S IN A BUILDING? 99

RISK TAKER AND TIMBER ENTREPRENEUR 103

ALBERT BAUR AND THE BANJO............. 107

SLEUTHING FOR CLUES........................ 111

THE VISUAL ARTISTS AMONG US 115

UNIQUE TO THIS PLACE 119

FROM TUBA PLAYER TO TYCOON 125

AWAITING COLLEGE 129

SOME GAVE THEIR LIVES...................... 133

GETTYSBURG AND THE 105th 137

OLD MACDONALD HAD A FARM 141

VERSATILITY WITH THE CAMERA LENS .. 145

THE SHACK CALLED BLUEBIRD BUNGALOW 149

GUESS WHO'S COMING TO BROOKVILLE? 153

"THE GO" OF BASEBALL IN BROOKVILLE 157

"CLIFF" DEEMER'S ORISKANY BUG......... 161

CLOTHES MAKE THE MAN!..................... 165

A 19th CENTURY ARTIST'S WORK 169

EXHIBITIONIST, BARNSTORMER, OR EXHIBITION FLYER? 173

DANCING THE NIGHT AWAY................... 177

BE MY VALENTINE................................. 181

FROM MAN TO MYTH............................ 185

BOWDISH WRITES 191

SPACES FOR SPORT 195

LAST ONE IN IS A ROTTEN EGG!............ 199

THAT LONG FOOTBALL HIATUS.............203

HOW WILL YOU SPEND NEW YEAR'S EVE?
....209

REMEMBER WHEN GIRLS WORE
BLOOMERS?....................................213

FLITTING, A RITE OF SPRING.................217

GOOGLING THE COLUMBIA....................221

A PAST PANDEMIC.............................227

HAIL TO THE CHIEF!...........................231

WHEN THE PRIDE OF THE WOODS BLOOMS
IN JUNE...235

THEIR HIGHNESSES, THE LAUREL QUEENS
....239

BROOKVILLE'S "POSTER CHILD" AND THE
MYSTERY OF THE MISSING CORNERSTONE
....243

LITTLE LEAGUE BASEBALL IN BROOKVILLE
....247

BROOKVILLE SAYS MERRY CHRISTMAS!.251

WHAT DO YOU DO AT A HISTORY CENTER?
....255

INDEX...259

PREFACE

HOW MANY WORDS IN HISTORY?

Remember when the teacher would write a long word on the board, maybe a spelling word, and students would go to work with paper and pencil to identify the little words in the big word? For instance, H-I-S-T-O-R-Y? *Is*? *His*? *To*? *Rot*? How about *story*?

Our definition of history, a subject plenty of folks found dull in school, is "the stories of change over time." Those stories may be as national as the stories of the presidency and how our democracy has changed. Or they may be local, the stories of families in Jefferson County and how they changed from the time they arrived, through the heydays of timbering in the nineteenth century and the Great Depression in the twentieth, to how they live and what they value in the twenty-first century.

At the Jefferson County History Center we use objects, photographs, and documents to tell the stories that show change over time right here in this place where we live. We do it through exhibits. We do it through public programs. And we do it through publications.

In 2006 the *Brookville Mirror* and *County Neighbors* newspapers invited us to write monthly columns. Our readers tell us they find these pieces interesting, so we have collected three years of columns into this book and hope you will enjoy them as you pick and choose to read about the people, places, and events of Jefferson County. We most certainly have enjoyed writing about them.

Carole A. Briggs
Curator

OUR NATIVE AMERICANS AND THE SENECA

The History Center's 2007–2008 award-winning exhibit, *Native American Lifeways in Western Pennsylvania*, showed evidence of five cultures that lived in this region centuries ago with conclusions about how they lived. During exhibit planning sessions, we wrestled with questions of content and terminology—what major points of view to include? Should the exhibit be open-ended? What terms would we use? For example, contributors used *group, tribe, tradition,* and *culture* to refer to the long ago people who made and used the objects now seen in our exhibit cases.

When problems like these arise our first source is that old favorite—Webster's dictionary. There we find *culture*—the customary beliefs, social forms, and material traits of a racial, religious, or social group. *Tradition*—the handing down of information, beliefs, and customs by word of mouth or by example from one generation to another without written instruction. *Tribe*—a group of persons having a common character, occupation, or interest, and *group*—a number of individuals assembled together or having some unifying relationship.

Native American web sites, too, offer help. For example, when reading about the Iroquois Confederation, the groups that came together sometime between 1450 and 1570AD (or perhaps as early as 900 according to some sources) under the legendary Hiawatha, we learn that the five original Indian tribes of the Confederation were the Mohawk, Oneida, Onondaga, Cayuga, and the Seneca.

But four of the five Native American groups depicted in our exhibit predated the formation of the Iroquois Confederation. Who were they? What happened to them? Did they become part of the Confederation when it formed? A recent history of Pennsylvania includes a map showing Native American groups that existed around 1550. They are the Monongahelas to the south; the Eries, Susquehannocks, and Iroquois to the north; and the Munsees, Shenk's Ferry People, and Lenapes to the east. In our area, the area east of the Allegheny River and south of the Clarion, are the words "Poorly Known Groups."

While we might have used the term *group* we decided to call these people *cultures.* And so the exhibit featured objects from the Allegheny Iroquois Culture (940—1525AD), Mead Island Culture (970—1300AD), Fishbasket Culture (1050—1250AD), Monongahela Culture (1109—1452AD), and McFate Culture (1450—1580AD).

With the arrival of Columbus, the Jamestown settlers, and the Pilgrims, the period of contact started. Native Americans and Europeans traded goods, learned from each other, intermarried, and competed for land. *Pennsylvania: A History of the Commonwealth* (2002) adds, "Viruses from Europe may well have been the first living things to reach interior villages from across the Atlantic." Within a century, it is estimated that 75 to 95% of many cultures had died from smallpox, measles, and influenza, forcing the survivors to "recombine, resettle, and recoalesce into new entities."

We do know that when Joseph Barnett arrived with his family, there were very few Native Americans in this area. County historian Kate Scott quotes his daughter, "When we came to Port Barnett, in the spring of 1797, there were but two Indian families there. One was Twenty Canoes, and Caturah, which means Tomahawk. The two Hunts were here, but they were alone. Jim Hunt was on banishment for killing his cousin. Captain Hunt and Jim Hunt were cousins. Captain Hunt was an under-chief of the Munsey (sic) tribe. In the fall other Indians came here to hunt. I have forgotten their names, with the exception of two, John Jamieson, who had seven sons, all named John; the other was Crow, he was an Indian in name and in nature. He was feared by both the white and Indians. He was a Mohawk...."

Today it is not uncommon for folks to visit the research room at the History Center intent upon tracing their Native American heritage. Indeed, as Native American pride has swelled, census records show an increase in the number of people claiming that heritage. We direct them to the nearest source of information, the Allegheny Indian Reservation at Salamanca, New York, an area where 7,200 Senecas live today.

When the colonists or rebels revolted against the British, the tribes of the Iroquois Confederation were told they could choose whom they would follow. Four fought with the British, and two, the Onondagas and Tuscarawas, with the colonists. Captain Joseph Brant, a Native American, led both Iroquois and British soldiers. After the Revolution, many of the Senecas who had fought with the British followed colonial loyalists into Canada, but one group settled around Buffalo, New York.

Might the descendants of those "Poorly Known Groups" have joined these Senecas? Perhaps. Or might they have traveled south and merged with the Monongahelas? Perhaps? Or north to the Mohawks? We do not know. Perhaps future archaeologists will provide the answer.

Visitors at the Jefferson County History Center enjoy the roundhouse model created by field archaeologist Ken Burkett.   *JCHS Photograph*

NO MATTER THE NAME
1797

County historians called them shanties, wigwams, cabins, or houses. What were these early dwelling places like in Jefferson County?

The Native Americans who crisscrossed the region lived in roundhouses. Ken Burkett, who documented the Fishbasket site just across the county line in Armstrong and Clarion Counties, found evidence of the posts used to frame these roundhouses as well as storage pits of varying sizes, but evidence of just one longhouse. Native Americans to the north of us built the longhouses commonly depicted in descriptions of the Iroquois.

When the first descendants of Europeans arrived in the late 18th century, the first priority was clearing enough land to plant corn. These first families may have built temporary structures of tree limbs and bark similar to those constructed by the Native Americans, until time permitted a more permanent structure to be raised. But there were no house plans for purchase! No architects to hire! What they built depended upon what they knew. And what they knew were the homes they'd left behind.

The Swedes who settled along the Delaware River in the 1600s used the same "log cabin" patterns for building that they'd used in Sweden. According to architectural historians, the English, Scots, Germans, Irish, and French learned log construction techniques from the Swedes and from the Finns as well.

5

This form of construction used no nails, just logs placed horizontally, yet the houses provided protection through the cold of winter. Logs for the very first homes were cut with a simple saddle notch for cornering. A curved notch was made in the bottom of round logs and the upper log "rode" on the lower log. Like Lincoln logs, these logs protruded from the corners. For later structures, bark was removed on two or more sides and corner notches varied.

According to Tom Brandon, who has documented many old log structures in Western Pennsylvania, the corner notches of the remains of log structures found in Jefferson County are indicative of two different groups of people. In the north where the Scots-Irish dominated, builders used the ½ dovetail and square notch. In the south where German descendants settled, the "V" notch predominated. Other corner notches are the double notch, square, steeple, and round.

McKnight describes these first cabins as small, perhaps fifteen or sixteen feet square, and one or one and a half stories high with a ladder to the sleeping loft. As the population grew, more people were around to help with building a house. On the first day of a house-raising, materials were gathered including puncheons for the floor and clapboards for the roof. Men used broadaxes to smooth the face of split logs for floor puncheons. Stones outlined the cabin perimeter.

The next day the four "corner men" began the job of notching the logs and laying them atop each other. As soon as the walls were "a few rounds high" others began laying puncheons for the floor. Men cut a three-foot wide opening for the door and a wider opening at one end for the chimney. They might cut a window opening, too, that would be covered with greased paper.

When the walls were high enough, two longer end logs were laid to support the butting poles that would support the clapboards for the roof. The logs on the shorter sides were cut shorter and shorter to form the angled roof. Masons made mortar to daub or "chink" the cracks and build the chimney.

The third day, men added a two-part door and some furnishings. A split slab on four logs made a table. Log pins stuck between the logs supported shelving. A single forked branch driven into a hole in the floor, and poles laid on the forked branch with the opposite ends forced into the chinked spaces created a bed frame.

Joseph Barnett built his log cabin on Mill Creek in 1797. Moses Knapp built his log house in 1801 at the mouth of the North Fork. Other families arrived and built cabins and mills. Brookville was laid out in June of 1830 and by August the first house appeared at the corner of Main and Spring alley. By this time, mills provided boards for houses made of "frame timbers, mortised and tenoned, and fastened with oak pins.". That same year stonemason and bricklayer Thomas Barr came to town to make the bricks for the new jail and courthouse and houses, too. The days of the pioneer log cabins were over.

According to Brandon, the oldest log structure existing in the county today is more than likely a spring house in the Beechwoods area that was built sometime between 1826 and 1840.   Photographer Tom Brandon

THERE'S NO PLACE LIKE
A SHANTY
1797—1830

Brookville was a "town of shanties" when McKnight wrote his childhood memoir that covered the years 1840 to 1843 "when my feet were bare and my cheeks were brown." He included it in his two-volume history printed in 1917.

The word "shanty" may be derived from two sources. The French word "chantier" in Canada means a lumber camp. An Ohio source in 1820 describes people living in a shanty—an 8x10 foot hovel. Or it may be derived from the Irish *sean tig*, "old house," supposedly supported by the large numbers of expatriate Irishmen who were employed on projects and lived in the earliest *shanty towns*.

No matter the derivation, we know daily life in a shanty could not have been easy. McKnight's memoir describes it quite well.

Unlike the first small log homes built by the earliest settlers, these shanties were put together with "frame timbers, mortised and tenoned, and fastened with oak pins, as irons and nails were scarce, people being poor and having little or no money." Soap-making, dying, and some cooking were done in the back yard where there would be an "out-oven," an "ash-hopper," a "dye kettle," and "a rough box fastened to the second story of the necessary, in which to raise early cabbage plants." The "necessary," of course, was the outhouse or toilet facility. The garden included the usual vegetables as well as catnip, peppermint, sage and tansy, herbs used by the woman of the house for dying, cooking, and medicinal purposes.

Inside the shanty, women cooked over a fireplace. A crane swung in and out over the fire and nearby were the poker, tongs, and a shovel for removing ashes. The crane included a set of rods of different lengths so kettles could be suspended at the proper height. Mothers used a long-handled frying pan, a short-handled three-legged "spider," and a griddle. They used a "bake-kettle," a kettle with a tight-fitting lid and legs to bake the daily corn pone. A split broom handled the sweeping.

The earliest tableware was perhaps whittled from wood unless a few treasures of pewter or iron had been carried over the mountains. Knives and forks made of iron with bone handles and china came later.

Some of our early pioneers brought furniture with them. Others built their tables, stools, and beds from materials at hand. For those early pioneers living in log cabins, one method of building a bedstead was to use the corner of the room and place a forked branch in the dirt floor as the bed's fourth corner post. Poles could then extend from the forked branch into the spaces between the log walls. These poles would make the "springs," upon which lay the bedding—a tick filled with straw or corn shocks, a quilt or hap, and pillows stuffed with down. The folks living in the shanties on Main Street most likely used a roped bedstead.

The family's clothing hung on pegs or perhaps was stored in a trunk. Like the "ash-hopper" and "dye kettle," spinning wheels for both flax and wool were important household items, as were hackles, cards, niddy-noddies, reels, and perhaps even a loom.

When not in use, the trusty musket or flintlock may have been displayed over the fireplace. The fireplace provided some light, of course, and other light perhaps came through a window covered with oiled-paper, from a "Betty lamp," or from dipped or molded candles. McKnight mentions the candle stands were made of tin, iron, or brass, and made with a broad, flat base, turned up to catch the grease. Families used a "snuffer" to extinguish the flame and to clip the charred wick. Matches weren't available until after the 1830s so banking the fire at night and blowing to revive it in the morning were twice-daily activities.

An early log house built of squared timbers and possibly inhabited by ancestors of Minerva Harding.
Donation of John & Esther DeMotte, Brookville

Houses built during the decade preceding the Civil War often included elements of Federal architecture, like the small windows around the doorway of the Oliver Brady homestead in Pinecreek Township. The house burned in 1940.
Photographer Unknown
JCHS Collection

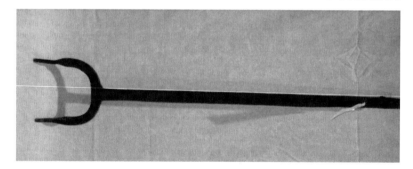

Pete Spratt, Sigel, has loaned the History Center a long-handled three-legged trivet that he found along the Clarion River. We might imagine a woman using it to place a pot closer to the coals in the fireplace at the end of her cabin.

TOOLS FOR TIMBER
1797—1830

With ax and maul and wedge they set out to wrest from this new life the economic security denied them in the place whence they had come." So wrote Wright and Corbett in their 1940 book *Pioneer Life,* a handy source about frontier life in southwestern Pennsylvania.

Wright and Corbett used multiple original sources related to southwestern Pennsylvania to describe the lives of these hardy pioneers. Here in Jefferson County, our sources aren't as numerous. So where do we find clues about the tools these adventuresome frontier folks might have used here in our county?

Fortunately the collection at the History Center does include some 19th century tools—those wonderful handmade pieces that show the years of their use. We don't know an awful lot about when they were used or who used them, but perhaps with a little sleuthing we can surmise a bit!

Ax blades go back to the Stone Age when humans first figured out how to sharpen certain kinds of stone that could then be used to shape wood, cut hides, and even shape softer stone. Then somewhere down the long lane of time, a crafty individual figured out how to attach an antler to the blade for a handle, and finally, during the Iron Age, those early smithies learned to craft blades out of iron.

When the first pioneers ventured westward along the west branch of the Susquehanna there is little doubt that they would have included an ax, a maul, and a wedge among their belongings because these three tools would be vital to the construction of the first shelter. The ax would fell the saplings that, when covered with canvas, would provide the temporary shelter required while the first cabin or shanty was under construction.

With the arrival in 1830 of the first blacksmith, William McCullough, local folks could be supplied with things of metal. McCullough located his blacksmith shop and home on the land where the present Baptist Church now stands. According to Eric Sloane who has written extensively about the things of early America, the ax-making process was the same until the end of the 19th century. First an iron pattern was folded. Then a steel wedge was added before both were hammered over a metal handle pattern. Then the metal handle pattern was replaced with a handle of wood.

Sloan describes many kinds of axes; felling axes, broad axes, mortise axes, and chisel axes, each with distinct characteristics. Clearing the land for the first crops took precedence and this required a felling ax. The ax could cut a saddle-notch or sharp-notch in the longest log one man could handle, probably about sixteen-feet long.

With a broad ax, a log could be "squared." Then using a maul, mortise ax, and saw, square-notch corners could be used to build a better structure.

To split rails for fencing, these pioneers used a maul to pound and an oak or iron wedge.

Exchanging the wedge for a froe, the same technique was used to split a block of wood into shingles, barrel staves, or clapboards.

Saws became important, too. Greek mythology credits Perdix, the nephew of Daedalus, with the invention of the hand saw, and folks at Colonial Williamsburg say the tool is more than 5,000 years old. According to the myth, Perdix walked on the beach where he picked up the spine of a fish. He copied the notched shape to a piece of iron and invented the hand saw. Examples of notched blades made of bronze have been found around the world as well.

Woodworkers in colonial America used both frame and large open saws to cut planks, boards, and veneers and smaller saws for cutting smaller pieces, joints and decorative piercings. Early saws used by individuals included ripsaws, handsaws, compass saws, back saws, bow saws, and felloe saws. The cross-cut or pit saw was used by two men. The man above had the harder job as he pulled and guided the saw that cut the log.

Sloane writes "to *buck* logs was to saw them into proper lengths; hence, the buck saw is a woodsman's saw." Consisting of a handle, arms, brace, winding stick, blade, and rope, a buck saw is collapsible and very portable!

Timber men from New England arrived in Jefferson County in the 1830s and built mills where water power replaced human energy before being replaced by steam power. Prior to the Civil War, there were twenty-two on the North Fork producing ten million board feet annually, twenty on the Sandy Lick producing ten million

15

feet, and fifteen on the Red Bank and Little Sandy cutting 3,500,000 feet. Historian Scott estimated that these fifty-seven Jefferson County mills were sending 23,500,000 feet of boards down river each year. The timber industry had begun and the "economic security" sought by those early pioneers who had arrived with ax and maul and wedge was being achieved.

Men, women and children kept the double-bit axes sharp by turning grindstones like this one.
Photographer Frederick E. Knapp
Courtesy Brookville Heritage Trust

FARMING WITHOUT JOHN DEERE
1797—1900

Traveling the back roads among the county's Amish settlements gives a person a sense of what farming might have been like before the days of the gasoline-powered engine. Horse drawn plows turn the fields. Seeds drop into the soil from corn planters or by hand. Stacks of hay dot the hillsides.

Historians estimate that our pioneer farmers could prepare an acre for corn and a half acre for vegetables before the first winter arrived. Then each season more trees were girdled or felled, more fields were tilled, and farms became larger. By 1850 Jefferson County boasted 56,850 acres of "improved land." A little more than twice that acreage was unimproved. Thirty years later, there were 2,567 farms and 154,636 acres of "improved" land. That's nearly a three-fold increase!

When the first settlers of European descent arrived around 1800 Native Americans in the area were growing patches of corn. It became an important crop and important food, so much so that historian William J. McKnight wrote that "pone was not used more than thirty days in the month."

The vegetable we enjoy so much during August and September provided not only pone, hominy, mush, and johnnycake, but fuel, toys, corn cob pipes, and bedding. The ½ acre vegetable patch provided pumpkins, squash, beans, potatoes, cabbage, turnips, muskmelon, and wa-

17

termelon. By 1830 oats had far outstripped the bushels of wheat, rye, buckwheat, flax, and corn the county produced with potatoes a close second.

Planting these crops required tools. First, perhaps just a rudimentary hoe or even a stick to work the soil, then wooden shovels and hoes. A pioneer may have fashioned a crude wooden plow that could furrow soft ground, and if he'd been wealthy enough to arrive with oxen or horses, he could use animal power rather than his own or his wife's energy to pull it.

About the same time our pioneer farmers were clearing and tilling 1 out of every 3 acres of land, Charles Newbold, David Peacock, and Jethro Wood were patenting cast-iron plows in New Jersey and New York. It is interesting to note that some early farmers thought metal plows "poisoned the soil" and encouraged weeds!

Thomas Jefferson designed a moldboard plow for use at Monticello and later incorporated more and more parts of metal into it. The moldboard of a sidehill plow is reversible making it very good for the rolling hills of Pennsylvania.

According to the U.S. Department of Agriculture it took 40-50 labor hours to produce 100 bushels of wheat on five acres with a gang plow, seeder, harrow, binder, thresher, wagons, and horses in the 1890s. Gang plows were pulled by horses and made several furrows at a time, speeding up the process. Harrows and cultivators broke up the soil.

Raising and harvesting 100 bushels of corn took 35-40 labor hours on 2.5 acres with a two-bottom gang plow, disk and peg-tooth harrow, and 2-row planter. And that was in 1890, imagine the time and labor in 1830!

Reaping required a cutting tool. In the 1820s the sickle and scythe which let a man cut a half acre a day were replaced by the American grain cradle, a more upright way to get the job done. "Fingers" were attached to the *snath* or handle of the scythe making possible large sweeps across the grain. Then a man could reap 2 acres of wheat in a day.

Farmers used a flail to separate the grain from the stalk and later, horses would do the job by walking over the cut grain. Finally, the grain would be separated from the chaff by tossing it in the air, a process called winnowing.

By the end of the 19th century farming was on the way to the mechanization we see today. Reapers, threshers, and combines had been invented. Farmers were experimenting with stream-driven tractors. Fertilizer was in common use and agricultural production increased.

Jefferson County farms kept up with the technological changes in farm tools and by the early 1900s they, too, were using these new inventions to reduce the manual labor of farming that characterized the 19th century.

By the time of the 1880 census there were 2,567 farms in the county and 154,636 acres of "improved" land. Those farmers worked hard and earned an estimated $17M that year when recalculated in today's dollars. In 2002 there were 548 farms in the county and 86,899 acres in farmland, a substantial reduction. Farm income is a bit more than $12M. In other words, today fewer farmers farm less land than more than a century ago, but earn about 33% more per acre! And thanks to improvements in farm tools, with much less manual labor!

Farmers used an early steam or gasoline-powered threshing machine when they brought in crops near Western Avenue in the early part of the 20th century.
Photographer Frederick E. Knapp
Courtesy Brookville Heritage Trust

JEFFERSON COUNTY'S JOHNNY APPLESEED

FUDGEON VAN CAMP

1800—1801

Fudgeon Van Camp arrived in Jefferson County on his hands and knees. Back in Easton in 1800 or 1801 he and two friends, Stephen Roll and August Shultz, had heard "glowing accounts" of the Port Barnett settlement. Foolishly they left Easton in winter without food. Historian Kate Scott writes that they had reached the west branch of the Susquehanna when a storm covered the ground with two feet of snow making travel difficult. Roll and Shultz gave up, but Van Camp, the strongest of the three, trudged on. When he arrived at the Barnett shanty he told folks about the other two and a search party went out and found Roll. Looking further they finally found Shultz, who suffered the loss of four toes and eventually his life as a result of his winter travels.

Van Camp settled in Pinecreek Township on property along "the Ridgway road," north of farms established by Joseph McCullough and Nathaniel Butler. Today this is the area on Route 28 south of I-80. William Vasbinder's farm was to the north. Providentially Van Camp carried apple seeds on his overland journey, seeds that became the orchard on his farm of 218 acres. These original fruit trees were the first of many substantial orchards that developed.

According to McKnight, Van Camp was a very large man. A slave who served as a teamster

21

in the Revolutionary War, he purchased his freedom after the war. McKnight adds that other county pioneers who served in that war were Joseph and Andrew Barnett, Elijah Graham, and Joel Clarke. Might Van Camp have heard those "glowing accounts" from them?

Van Camp was a fiddler, too, who played for "all the early frolics," and McKnight adds "a great fighter." In 1810 court records show he was involved in a property dispute with his neighbor, Henry Vasbinder. It appears one was transgressing by tapping or harvesting maple trees that belonged to the other. The court established the creek or "run" as a line between the properties and ordered their neighbors, John Jones and Moses Knapp, to run the other property lines. Van Camp and Vasbinder were to "move their fence on their own ground" and leave a "lane or outlet" of sixteen feet and a half. The two were to promise to be on "their good behavior unto each other, their goods and chattles, for the term of one year and one day...."

Typically men came first to the frontier, built a shanty or cabin, then returned for their families. Joseph Barnett arrived in 1795 and returned with his family in 1797. Van Camp's wife died in Easton, and sometime before 1810 he returned there for his four children.

Census records show slow population growth in Jefferson County prior to the Civil War. Fudgeon Van Camp, our "Johnny Appleseed" was one among 161 people listed in 1810. He was older than 45 and had 5 or more other people living with him: a girl younger than 10, a boy between 10 and 16, and one boy and two girls between 16 and 26.

Prior to 1850 census records list only the head of household by name. These records also separate "free whites" from "coloreds" and "slaves." It is therefore unusual to find Sarah and Enos Van Camp listed by name in 1820 (Van Camp's other two children were Susan and Richard) when there were 561 people living here and 10 were listed as "colored." Van Camp, his four children and perhaps a child of Enos account for 6. We know from Scott and McKnight that Charles Southerland arrived about 1812 and he is listed with 2 others in his household. One cannot be identified.

Van Camp does not appear in the 1840 census but we have not located a record of his death. By then county population had grown to 7196 with 57 listed as "colored." Some like the Andersons, Douglasses, McGintys, Platos, and Southerlands, were families living in Eldred and Perry Townships and Brookville. Others like William Meed, Alexander Park, and an unnamed young woman lived with and worked for white families.

By 1850 there were nearly 100 "free blacks" living in Jefferson County, some the descendents of our "Johnny Appleseed." Enos married Rebecca and they lived in Rose Township with two young girls. Richard married Ruth Stiles, and their children married Entys. Like Fudgeon Van Camp, most earned their living by farming. Others like logger Henry Southerland were laborers. Joseph May worked in a Brookville hotel and Nathan Smith was a barber.

During February when we celebrate both the Black Americans among us and "Johnny Appleseed," too, we can appreciate that we are better-off today because of pioneers like Fudgeon Van Camp, Jefferson County's own "Johnny Appleseed," and his descendants.

Changed substantially over time, the home of Judge Elijah Heath at 64 Pickering Street once harbored fugitive slaves traveling north to Canada and freedom.
Photographer Frederick E. Knapp
Courtesy Brookville Heritage Trust

IN THE DEAD OF WINTER
1800—2008

Wintertime—the time of year when many of us turn into couch potatoes. We put Orville Reddenbacher Popcorn into the microwave, slip a movie into the DVD player, then bundle ourselves in a down comforter and forget the snows and winds of winter. We'd rather not think about shoveling sidewalks, school closings, or the possibility of falling and fracturing an ankle or hip. For others, however, the winter snow and ice raise thoughts of skiing and skating! How did folks a century ago deal with the dead of winter?

Weather has been of interest through the ages, but it took the development of scientific measuring systems and ways to rapidly communicate information before meteorology, or the science of weather, could come into its own. Penn State University offered a Geography and Meteorology course as early as 1859, but it took 75 years before a meteorologist taught it. Following the Civil War, President Grant instituted the National Weather Service, and the telegraph sped information along. During the 1930s and 1940s new scientific instruments made upper-level measurements possible, and with the development of computers and weather satellites, meteorology took off. Today we enjoy instant and constant information about weather conditions worldwide. It was not that way for much of the 19th century.

By 1865 our community could receive and send information about severe weather via telegraph, but word-of-mouth, traditional signs, and

25

the Farmer's Almanac predominated in weather forecasting! Like today, too, mentioning unusual weather was common. In her history, Scott refers to "a heavy snow storm" in 1800 or 1801 when Fudgeon Van Camp, Stephen Roll, and August Shultz traversed the mountains to get to Port Barnett. Newspapers in 1907 mentioned the "high wind" that blew down Mrs. Shofestahl's swinging millinery sign, smashing the plate glass front window "into atoms," and a Reynoldsville man who "sustained a fall on the ice, breaking his thigh." He was 93!

On the positive side, the cold and ice of February produced the "annual ice harvest ... that makes life worth living in the heat of summer." Later, melting snow caused the high water necessary for rafting, creating income for those who'd spent cold winter days cutting timber.

The winter of 1907 was relatively mild. People did get out and about until the icy days of early March. For entertainment, some participated in the YMCA bowling tournament and others danced at Pearsall Hall to music provided by the "St. Clair-Jelly Orchestra of Pittsburgh." People visited the "Theatorium" opposite the Jefferson Hotel (now the Scarlet Cord) to see an early form of moving pictures. Some, particularly single young adults, enjoyed sleigh riding, often traveling to nearby towns to meet friends.

Many awaited the opening of the new Casino Roller Skating Rink on Water Street (now Madison Street.) When it opened in late February, 600 people paid the admission fee and 300 skaters took to the maple wood floor, skating to music played by the Sons of Veterans Band.

People traveled by rail and motorcar. Mr. Carroll cranked up his White Steamer and drove to Tionesta. The Reverend James Conway and his wife traveled south to Florida leaving cold weather behind. R. M. Matson traveled south to check on his new timber interest there.

Weather affects road conditions, and in turn, road conditions affect school attendance, business and industry, and entertainment. In 1907 roads appeared to be passable and folks went about their daily routines. But that wasn't true in 1947. Even though the Department of Highways had increased by 101 the number of miles they would clean in Jefferson County, rural roads were left snow-covered.

Larry Aharrah grew up in Heath Township and attended the Wallace School. He remembers the winter of 1947 well. "I rode three mile to school on a bus pulled by horses....They didn't have snowplows to plow the roads like they do now, so they did have some trouble keeping the roads open for us....My brothers and I missed three weeks of school. They opened the roads with a bulldozer and two of my brothers went one day. I had a bad tooth and we went to town to the dentist. It snowed that night and we pretty near didn't get home. The next morning the roads were closed again, and we missed four more weeks. We missed seven weeks of school that winter!" In Brookville nearly forty percent of the students were absent for days due to high winds and drifts of five to ten feet that closed ninety percent of the county's secondary roads.

Today, even though we have instant knowledge about conditions worldwide and snow removal equipment ready, weather sometimes still has the upper hand and dictates how we spend our days in the dead of winter! So keep that package of popcorn handy!

Two clues in this photograph help date it to the dead of winter at the turn of the twentieth century; the large-sleeves of the women's jackets and the double span metal truss bridge on Pickering Street. That bridge was replaced by a single span metal truss bridge in 1905 after a flood the previous year had weakened the structure.
Photographer Frederick E. Knapp
Courtesy Brookville Heritage Trust

GROWING GREEN
1801—2001

Apple blossoms that dot the hillside near Jefferson Manor in the spring are a reminder of Fudgeon Van Camp, a man who came over the mountains to settle in Jefferson County. When he arrived from Easton during the winter of 1800—1801, he carried apple seeds, "this being the first effort to raise fruit in this wilderness," according to McKnight. The county historian goes on to describe Van Camp, Jefferson County's own Johnny Appleseed, as having hair as "white as the wool of a sheep" and a face "as black as charcoal." A widower, Van Camp raised two sons and two daughters and farmed just about where I-80 crosses SR28.

Trees have been a major part of our livelihood here in Jefferson County for more than two centuries, so perhaps it is appropriate in the spring to highlight people like Fudgeon Van Camp and their interest in trees.

Whether or not the earliest families to arrive here came to timber or farm is debatable for there is as much evidence supporting the one as for the other. Nevertheless, the fact remains that much of the county was covered with trees that had to be cut before a field could be planted. By 1900 much of the white pine and hemlock was gone, and stump-covered hillsides remained. Many lumbermen closed their mills and left to look for trees in Alabama, Georgia, Michigan, and the great northwest.

One timberman who stayed was Anthony Wayne Cook. His grandfather had arrived in 1826 at the eventual site of Cooksburg, then part of Jefferson County. John Cook, his son, and his grandson all timbered. Anthony Wayne eventually bought out Matson and Heidrick and ran the mill on the North Fork in Brookville. All three Cooks had been careful to preserve a large area of virgin pine timber near their Cooksburg homestead, and about the time the mill was ready to be torn down, "it became his ambition to save this magnificent heritage for the enjoyment of all the people for all time to come." Twenty-five years later, Anthony Wayne's persistent efforts resulted in the creation of Cook Forest State Park, now eight thousand acres of trees enjoyed by "all the people for all time to come."

In the 1930s, as second-growth hardwoods began to cover the hillsides once again, Congress created the Civilian Conservation Corps to provide work for the large numbers of unemployed young men. Here in Jefferson County, boys and young men lived in camps at the Hays Lot (S-53-Pa) and Sprankle Mills (SCS-2-Pa.) They planted trees, and built log cabins, trails, and bridges at Clear Creek State Park which we enjoy today.

Townspeople concerned themselves with trees, too. Brookville Borough Council created a shade tree commission in 1939. One of the first projects undertaken was the planting of trees on the "unused portion of Barnett Street between Jefferson and Jared streets," an area described as being in need of beautification. Other groups organized major plantings of crab apple trees.

When Historic Brookville, Inc. organized in 1983, the beautification of Main Street became part of its mission. The organization oversaw the installation of 19th century-looking light poles and brick insets in the sidewalks and tree wells. Much study went into determining which type of tree was appropriate for those tree wells.

Readers may recall the rededication of Dr. Walter Dick Memorial Park in 2001, five years after the disastrous flood destroyed the park first been dedicated in 1951, through the gracious gift of the Dick family. Long used as a swimming hole, the area had been planted with larch trees in 1947. Post-flood examination of the larches showed them to be diseased and dying, and they were removed to make way for the reconfigured park. Who would plant new trees? What species would they be? As part of the park project, the borough and the North Fork Watershed Association planted linden trees, a copper beech, Bradford pear, and other specimens.

Students plant trees, too. Hickory Grove Elementary School gets its name from the grove of shagbark hickories on the property. As the original trees began to die, former principal Fred Park arranged for students to plant new ones. Fourth graders planted fifteen in 1998. None survived. They were replanted the following year and five have survived.

We owe much to our forebears like Fudgeon Van Camp, A. W. Cook, the CCC men and boys, the Walter Dick family, students, and the many people who comprise tree commissions and watershed associations. These folks recognized then and recognize today the importance of trees in our daily lives, so it's appropriate in April when some trees begin to bloom and all put forth new leaves and needles, to thank these folks for their foresight so many years ago. Whether planted for food, their economic value, or their beauty, think of the people who planted trees in the past when you enjoy the green all around you this spring.

The Cook family preserved a large section of virgin forest north of Brookville in the 1920s. (Brookville Heritage Trust)

MISS MARTHA

1816—1898

Do you remember who taught you to read? That person who opened your eyes to the world of the printed page? And do you remember the little book you used in first grade? Some of us do with great fondness for both the book and the teacher. For others learning to read was more difficult—something hard to master. Consider the person, usually a woman, given the task of teaching a roomful of both eager and reluctant first graders. What skills did she bring to the classroom? How did she manage to succeed?

Martha McCreight was just sixteen when she began teaching in a subscription school in 1832, a school where families made the arrangements and paid the teacher directly. When Brookville Academy opened at the northwest corner of Jefferson and Barnett Streets in 1838, she began her many years of teaching Brookville boys and girls to read and to introducing them to school itself.

In 1946 Charlie Moore recalled what starting first grade was like for him. "It was in the fall of 1872, a day not to be forgotten. Georgia Romer had made me my first pair of pants; N. G. Edelblute furnished my first pair of coppertoed boots, and Mary Steff furnished the music by blowing on a comb to quiet me down for I would squawk and squall. I had lost my short dresses and deerskin moccasins and started on the way to school.

I would pull at the pants, get the boots under the old wooden sidewalk to pull them off, but finally I marched to the old academy on Jefferson street. I looked hard at the door, but a kind lady coaxed me in. She rang a bell—I have the same one yet! She held a pan up and says 'Listen' as she dropped a pin on it; they all heard it and then they all sang. Then she took a stick and pointed at some stuff on a board and Jim Richards began to cry, for she told him the big ball had the world on it where people lived and had all kinds of animals on it.

I thought so much of that same lady that I stayed two years...long live the memory of Martha McCreight!"

"Neighbor" Kennedy also had fond recollections of that first grade teacher. "On Friday afternoon Miss Martha always had the children recite little poems or a short piece that they had committed to memory. Oh, my what a time I had getting that speech in my head for my first Friday afternoon. But I got it in my mind so tight that it is there yet and the picture of that school room is so ground into my memory that it will never fade...."

By 1856 Brookville claimed four graded schools and by 1888, nine—four primary, three intermediate, and two grammar. "School" appears to indicate a classroom not a building. The school term was 8 months long, and Principal Galbraith supervised two male and seven female teachers who each earned between $36 and $65 a month. All but one, Martha McCreight, had fifteen years' experience or less. She had taught Primary 1 for 55 years and earned $36 a month.

The academy was condemned and torn down in 1877, and the new Central School was ready for public inspection Christmas Day 1878, with student occupancy happening later. There were also classes at the little one-room Longview building on Euclid Avenue and a small brick building on Franklin Avenue called Room Number Five. Miss Martha probably moved to Brookville's Central School where she continued to teach primary 1 until the 1892-1893 school year. She died in DuBois five years later and was buried in the new Brookville Cemetery.

During her sixty year teaching career, Martha McCreight used a variety of readers. Beginning with McGuffey Readers, she went on to use Osgood, Independent, Monroe, and Raub readers, but no matter the textbook, her students succeeded. Historian Scott wrote in 1888, "Nearly all the youth of the town have learned their A, B, C at her hands, and many of those who are now middle-aged have been her pupils. She is especially fitted for the position she has so long filled."

Nearly fifty years after her death Brookville graduates representing the classes of 1886 (the first graduating class) to 1946 gathered at the Northside Elementary Building to dedicate a brass plaque in her memory. Her obituary had stated she was "remarkably successful as a teacher, winning the respect and affection of her pupils, never to lose it." Those that had learned to read under her tutelage did remember her with affection on that day.

Martha McCreight, middle row, left, about 1880, is pictured with other teachers in the Brookville Public Schools.
JCHS Collection

When H. H. "Neighbor" Kennedy, one of Miss Martha's students, reached adulthood, he wrote several articles for a local paper recalling things of his past, including his first day in Miss Martha's first grade class.
Photographer Frederick E. Knapp
Courtesy Brookville Heritage Trust

WHY VICTORIAN?

1818—1901

Queen Victoria was a British monarch, not an American, so why is the term, "Victorian," used to describe this town of 4,500 in Jefferson County? Why is Brookville promoted as Historic Victorian Brookville?

Nineteen-year old Princess Victoria came to the British throne in 1837 upon the death of her childless uncle, William IV, the son of George III, and reigned until her death in 1901. During her 63-year-long reign, the longest in British history, it was said, "The sun never sets upon the British Empire." The Age of Discovery had begun with Columbus, and over the next centuries Britain grew into a power on the high seas. By the beginning of Victoria's reign Britain had colonies in North and South America, Asia, and Africa, as well as the entire Australian continent. Each morning the sun did indeed rise in turn over England, Ireland, Canada, Jamaica, British Guiana, New Zealand, Australia, Hong Kong, Malaysia, Burma, India, and South Africa—all British colonies.

Her reign was characterized by a strong work ethic, family values, religious observance, and institutional faith—beliefs some term "Victorian" or passé today. Thanks to inventions of the period like the sewing machine and improvements in wood-turning lathes, it was a time of exuberance, complexity, and great detail. Fashionable women wore ruffles and bows and homes were decorated with gingerbread!

When Victoria first wore the British crown, Americans were busy moving west. Between 1795 and 1850, Jefferson County's population had grown to more than 13,000 people, and even though many of their forebears had revolted against the British in 1776, some of these newcomers to the county subscribed to British magazines and papers and were influenced mightily by British styles and customs. We know, for example, from newspapers found in the rafters of the History Center that someone subscribed to and was reading the *Illustrated London News* in the summer of 1851.

As the northeast section of the United States moved from its agrarian beginnings to industrialization, a broad middle class emerged—entrepreneurs with money to spend on their homes and their families. Their homes, individually owned and landscaped with trees and shrubs, symbolized progress and family stability—it was the American dream come true.

In Brookville, timber and coal were making men wealthy. They, too, looked to spending their wealth on their homes and families, and just as British industrialization during Victoria's reign resulted in a variety of architectural styles, a variety of those styles is repeated in and around Brookville, and most buildings erected in Brookville between about 1840 and the twentieth century can accurately be described as "Victorian."

The History Center is indebted to Taylor and Taylor Associates, Inc. for their assistance in preparation of this article. Brookville, Pennsylvania: A Historic Architectural Coloring Book, *published by Historic Brookville, Inc. is available at the Jefferson County History Center.*

Greek Revival homes like the Hall-Nicholson-Arthurs home built in 1848 follow the timeless style of Greek architecture and include triangular pediments and columns like these topped with Ionic or scrolled capitals.

The Italianate Darrah house was built between 1860 and 1870. These homes were large, two to three stories tall, and characterized by low or hip roofs, wide corniced eaves supported by ornamental brackets, bay windows, and double-hung windows. Columns often framed the double entrance doors.

This three-storied asymmetrical structure, built between 1860 and 1890, is a good example of "stick" construction. The wooden wall cladding (in this case clapboards or board-and-batten siding) is interrupted by patterns of horizontal and vertical boards or stickwork that are raised from the wall surface for emphasis and are meant to represent the underlying framework. This style also featured multiple porches, paired windows, and steeply pitched roofs.

Steamboat or carpenter Gothic styles like the Hunt-Wolford house built about 1873 emerged prior to the Civil War. They are identified by steeply pitched roofs, steep cross gables, arched windows, vertical board and batten siding, one story porches, and "gingerbread." The floor plan is assymetrical.

French Second Empire structures like the Presbyterian manse built by R B. Taylor in 1884 are characterized by their boxy shape and Mansard roof. The inspiration came from the reign of Napoleon III, the French emperor from 1852 to 1870.

Towers, turrets, and wrap-around porches define the style called Queen Anne, along with elaborate dormers, windows, and chimneys. The style was popular in the United States between 1880 and 1910. Lawyer Cadmus Gordon built his home about 1890.

HERE COME THE JUDGES
1821–2008

Since 1869 the Jefferson County court-room has undergone many changes. Clear panes have replaced the original stained glass windows and today's technology has solved the acoustical problem mentioned by historian Kate Scott.

But just like your rooms at home, court-rooms accumulate things. During renovations things are removed, some replaced, others stored. Following the most recent renovation, portraits were taken down, cleaned, conserved, and then some were rehung. Plaques were polished. Today the refurbished courtroom is an exquisite interior. But who are those faces that peer down on judge and jury? Who was Katherine Rogers?

In 1986 the Jefferson County Bar Association honored Katherine Rogers (1906—1991) for fifty years of service as assistant to the president judge. She began her service under Judge Long in 1936 and continued under Judges Morris and Snyder before retiring in 1987. Efficient and quiet, she was a well-respected professional in court circles.

The portraits that now grace the walls are some of the president judges who presided over court here and who were born or later lived in the county, the first portrait being William Parsons Jenks. For much of the 19th century Jefferson County was linked with other counties to form a judicial district, first with Potter, McKean, and Warren. Later when Elk and Forest were

45

formed out of Jefferson County, those three along with Venango and Clarion formed the 18th Judicial District. Most judges during those early years were born in and lived in other counties.

William P. Jenks (1821—1902) the first president judge native to Jefferson County was educated at home and attended Jefferson College (now Washington and Jefferson) before studying law under his elder brothers. He was admitted to the bar, appointed district attorney at the age of 24, and elected to the state assembly in 1866 to represent Clarion and Jefferson Counties. In 1871 Jenks was elected president judge of the 18th Judicial District (Clarion, Jefferson, Forest Counties). McKnight writes that "During his term the discovery of oil in the district, and the shifting of the center of oil production toward it, rendered it for a while one of the busiest and most important districts in the state. The controversy between the producers and the pipeline interests, involving, as it did, railway transportation problems and the system of secret rebates, centered there for a time. His insistence that both sides come out into the open cost him dear personally, but, at a time when both lawyers and business men throughout the country were groping more or less blindly for a solution, it helped point the only way by which justice could be secured."

Jenks was followed by James B. Knox (Tioga Co.), William L. Corbet (Clarion), Theophilus S. Wilson (Clarion), and W. W. Barr (Clarion), who all served less than the ten-year term adopted as part of the 1851 state constitution.

46

Elijah Heath Clark (1839—1909) was born in Brookville, attended school there and then academies in Saltsburg and New Bethlehem. He read law under George W. Ziegler and the Jenks brothers before being admitted to the bar in 1866. Elected president judge of the 18th Judicial District (Clarion and Jefferson Counties) in 1891, he served until 1895 when the county was declared the 54th Judicial District of Pennsylvania. Judge Clark continued as the president judge of Clarion County. Since then all president judges have been residents of the county. President Judge John W. Reed (1853–1926) was born in Clarion and educated there. He studied law under James Campbell while teaching school, and after being admitted to the bar in 1875, began his practice in Brookville. He spent a year in Grand Forks, Dakota, before returning to the firm of Wilson and Jenks. Upon his return he became the Republican candidate for judge of the newly created 54th Judicial District. Governor Hastings appointed him to that position, and he was successful in the fall election and again in the election of 1905. He was renown in criminal practice and ran an "economical administration." McKnight writes that he was defeated in 1915 "in the clash of opinion regarding judicial and legislative responsibility in the no-license question." Supported by the brewers, saloons, and corporations, he lost the election by fewer than 600 votes.

President judges in the 20th century include Charles Corbet, William Thompson Darr, Jesse C. Long, Robert Means Morris, Edwin Snyder, William L. Henry, and the current president judge, John H. Foradora

William P Jenks
Served 1871-81

Elijah Heath Clark
Served 1891-95

John Reed
Served 1895-1915

Charles Corbet
Served 1916-26

William Thompson Darr
Served 1926-36

Robert Means Morris
Served 1950-72

Jesse C. Long
Served 1936-50

Edwin Snyder
Served 1972-92

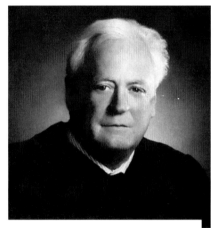

William C. Henry
Served 1992-2002

*Courthouse Portraits
Photographed by
Biandi Photography & Arts*

WATER, WATER, EVERYWHERE!
1828

Ask an older person in Jefferson County if they remember the flood and they may answer the question with a question, "Whiche one—'96 or '36?" Both years were marked with significant flooding in Jefferson County and throught

Out Pennsylvania as a whole. March 17th marks the anniversary of the St. Patrick's Day Flood of 1936 and July 19th marked the anniversary of the flood of 1996. Both events caused significant damage, and both were well-recorded by the local press.

Our river systems can wreak havoc, but they were also extremely important to the timber industry of the 19th century. Rivers in Jefferson County other than the Clarion on the northern border are shallow so the movement of timber was limited to times of high water. In fact, timberman Thomas K. Litch developed a system for artificially creating flood conditions in order to move logs, timber, and lumber down river. We think Litch invented the bracket dam system, and thanks to William McCracken's model of a bracket dam on exhibit in the History Center, we are able to show folks how it worked.

Historian Kate M. Scott cites many freshets and running the logs as well as times of high water that were memorable for other reasons. In her book, *History of Jefferson County, Pennsylvania*, she lists "high flood" mad rushing tor-

51

rents'" that occurred in 1828, 1832, 1847, 1861, 1865, and 1884.

We wonder what happened to the "fine Photographic views of the late Freshet" taken by young photographer E. C. Hall. According to a news snippet in the March 1865 newspaper, he'd taken pictures of "the covered bridge, with the buildings on the opposite side; another of a fine view of Brown & Wahnn's Foundry, the residence of Mr. J. E. Brown, Bridge, etc. surrounded by water; the third shows Taylor's Grist Mill surrounding buildings, with the angry waters sweeping around them." Might these images biding in an attic somewhere?

The "disastrous flood" of 1884 occurred on June 10th following hard rains and causing great worry to three lumber companies with logs in the North Fork. At eight o'clock in the evening torrents of water swept the logs, rudges, and footbridges downstream, and the next morning the lumbermen claimed losses of $60,000. No lives were lost but one employee at the Litch Mill was stranded on an Island in the North Fork, "about one hundred and fifty feet from the fnearest shore. One effort after another to get a line to him failed, and it began to be fearded that he could not be got off. The current was too swift to think of swimming, and Mr. Rankin was too numb and cold to attempt it. Finally at about eleven o'lclock, the men on short succeeded in throwing him a line and getting him safely on shore, but so cold and stiff that he could scarcely walk."

Certainly such an event would be cause for concern in a community as well as thanksgiving upon the safe rescue. Sadly, not all floods are victimless.

America's greatest flood disaster of the 19th century occurred the year after Scott's book was published. When the South Fokr Dam above Johnstown broke on May 31st, 1889, a wall of water sixty feet high coursed through the narrow valley at forty miles per hour. 2,2000 died within ten minutes. As disastrous as the Johnstown Flood was, it was surpassed by the hurricane and flooding that occurred in Galeston in 1900 when more than 8,000 people lost their lives.

The after-effects of hurricanes like the one that hit Galveston are sometimes felt as far north as Jefferson County. According to Penn State's flood monitoring data, all or most Pennsylvania counties were declared disaster areas following hurricanes Agnes (1972), Floyd (1996), Isabel/Henri (2003), Ivan (2004), and Katrina (2005).

In addition to the after effects of hurricanes, Jefferso County has also had isolated flooding. Allong with several other counties we witnessed flooding three times in 1974 and again in 1976, 1977, 1981, and 1996.

The memora le flood of 1996 affected eleven counties and, like the Johnstown Flood, was caused by supersaturated ground following unprecedented rainfall. In Brookville even the Federal Flood Control Project of Federal Flood Control Project of the 1950s and 1960s could not

53

contain the wall of water that spilled through the river valley when the earthen dam on the North Fork gave way

Throughout our history high water has been both a boon and a bane.

Looking north towards Brookville's Central School, high water spilled over the Red Bank during the St. Patrick's Day flood in 1936 and moved up White Street.

BROOKVILLE'S GREAT HALLS
1830

Once Brookville's Main Street was home to great halls, large spaces on the second or third stories of buildings, where entertainment events took place, organizations met, and speakers informed the citizenry. There was no radio, television, or Internet.

Most folks might think immediately of the Marlin Opera House (begun in 1883, the building where six commercial businesses are located on the first floor and a wide stairway leads to the second floor), but there were other large spaces on Main Street where crowds interacted. The

The first large space available for public gatherings after lots were sold on Main Street in 1830 was the jail. Presbyterians conducted services there until their church sanctuary was completed. When the courthouse itself was completed, the Methodists used it for worship.

Schoolhouses were other large spaces. In 1856 school superintendent Samuel McElhose decided to host an annual teachers' institute, and the first group met in a Punxsutawney "schoolhouse at candlelighting." Attendance grew and soon teachers were coming to Brookville for four and five days to listen to lectures and be entertained in the Courthouse, the Belvedere Opera House, and the Methodist Church.

How large were Brookville's great halls? In 1910 evidently not large enough to hold all the teachers expected for the annual event. County school superintendent Jones explained in a front-page article that the annual Teachers' Institute would be held in Reynoldsville that fall because the Belvedere owners had refused in 1909 and the Courthouse was too small. "As there is no other building that can be had we are compelled to seek a building elsewhere."

In response to that change, in 1914 community leaders began building the Brookville Park Auditorium Building. However, circumstances made its use for large events minimal over the following decades, and it became known as Brookville's "White Elephant."

People looked to large spaces for parties and dancing, too. In 1865 as the Civil War was winding down, there was a post-Christmas dinner and dance for 200 guests at the American House (rebuilt in 1857 and known later as the American Hotel) on Main Street.

Following the Civil War, John McCracken built what is now named Landmark Square on the southeast corner of Main and Valley streets, a building Scott describes as containing "two stores, and the upper a large town hall, while the other rooms are occupied by private families." An itinerant stencil painter decorated the walls with murals depicting the Civil War and other military symbols. People danced in McCracken Hall, and in recent years, the custom was revived when the annual Victorian Ball took place there each December.

The county built a new courthouse in 1869, and the Central Hotel, the building that now houses a variety of shops and offices on the southeast corner of Main and Pickering, replaced the Franklin House, Nicholson Hall, and the Oak Hall Hotel, three structures that burned in the great fire of 1874.

Lodges and secret societies were phenomena of the early 19th century, and their large memberships required large meeting places. The meeting room of the Independent Order of Odd Fellows burned in the first of 1856. They surrendered their charter, but reorganized later and had their meeting room on the third floor of the Parker P. Blood Building (est. 1875) where the letters I.O.O.F. may still be seen high up on the building's façade. The Masonic Lodge moved from the American House to other spaces including Nicholson Hall, and finally located in the

McKnight Building (est. 1871) now the Courthouse Grill.

Finally, in 1883 Silas Marlin began to build what is the largest and best known of Brookville's great halls. The then-called Marlin Block contained a "splendid new hall" on the second and third floors, six retail spaces and eleven offices. This "large and elegantly fitted up opera house, with a seating capacity of over nine hundred" was used for a video documentary about Stephen Foster in 1999. Co-producer Randall MacLowry praised the hall. "The Marlin Opera House is an incredible artifact of American theater history." Between 1886 and 1902, Brookville's grandest hall was the setting for performances of all types, high school graduations, speakers, religious programs, and other types of entertainment.

Church sanctuaries and the courtroom continued to provide space for large audiences, and other large spaces appeared. Today, the high school auditorium seats more than 800. Fire halls, church halls, Grange halls, Hobah Lodge, and the YMCA all have large meeting spaces, too.

In the 21st century, we do turn to the latest in communication technology for much of our entertainment and information. But to watch a school play or hear a choral concert we still visit the large meeting spaces available in our community—church sanctuaries, school auditoriums, lodges, and fire halls—our great halls of today.

THE MILLINERS OF BROOKVILLE
1830–1950

Smaller than a breadbox, black, and made in Brookville. Can you guess what it is?

It's the hat that we think Brookville milliner Dora Sowers made. It's black velvet with feathers, and the tag that arrived with it said "Sowers". We think Dora made it because she was born in 1900, and the hat is typical of those worn after World War I.

Brookville was home to many milliners in the 19th and early 20th centuries, women who designed and made the hats women wore. Back then ladies wore hats whenever they left home—not just for worship, but for shopping and socializing, too.

Brookville's population grew from 276 in 1840 to 1,063 in 1850. We might estimate that about 200 were women, who had arrived with their families by covered wagon and survived a first winter in a lean-to, a relative's "shanty", or by living in one of the hotels. They'd helped their husbands cut timber, chinked the cabin walls, and planted crops to provide sustenance. As the family's clothing wore out, some wove new cloth on the family loom. Others bought fabric from Main Street merchants, and it wasn't long before they were buying hats from the local milliners.

Between 1830 when Brookville was established and 1860 at least three milliners worked to keep the town's women fashionable.

We know only their names: the Misses Ann Guffey, Ellen Butler, and S. A. McKillep. The milliner we know most about is Amelia F. Melchoir, the daughter of a German couple who arrived in Brookville in 1852. Amelia was twenty-five in 1868 when she took over Ellen Butler's millinery shop. She relocated several times and in 1874 married Civil War veteran John Wilson Henderson. Two years later her Main Street shop burned in the great fire.

In 1882 the Hendersons bought the brick building at 160 Main Street, built by Robert Barr. As was common, the Hendersons resided in this building, too. Amelia operated her "millinery and fancy goods" shops for more than fifty years. McCracken wrote in 1920 that she "has the distinction of having the oldest business concern now trading in town." Amelia died in 1923.

The "home news" and "home happenings" columns of local newspapers made a point of mentioning when local milliners traveled to Buffalo and Philadelphia to view the latest in fashions and to buy the materials needed to create hats for the coming season. Mrs. Henderson often took her assistant. Other milliners mentioned in newspapers and old directories include Mrs. Smith, Lena Jackson, Emma Paine Henry (Mrs. W. A.), and Mrs. Carroll. In fact, in the 1905-1906 directory it appears that four milliners had shops very near each other: the Aaron sisters at 140 W. Main; Amelia at 142 W. Main (the present state store renumbered as 160); Lena, an aunt of Addie Edelblute Pearsall, at 152

W. Main, now the History Center Shop and re-numbered as 172; and Mrs. Shofstahl at 166 W. Main, most likely where the Area Agency on Aging is now located.

Hats were important accessories well into the twentieth century. Women went to club meetings and charity organization events wearing dresses, hats, gloves, heels, and carrying a handbag. Ready made hats were available at least by 1918 when Mrs. Carroll's Woman's Shop advertised "city trimmed hats." Hatboxes in the History Center's collection are clues that Brookville women traveled to DuBois, Clearfield, and Pittsburgh to purchase hats. The last mention of a millinery shop occurs in the 1950 Brookville phone directory, though shops like Wein's and Rubin's did continue to sell hats.

Tracing the increase and decrease in hat size is interesting. Prior to the Civil War, women wore bonnets that tied underneath the chin. With eveningwear they wore headpieces or adornments of flowers, beads, and ribbon. Then bonnets disappeared and hats perched on the head, increasing in size until the turn of the century. When the nickelodeon appeared, so did cartoons with the line "Lady, please remove your hat!"

Then hat size diminished and during the Roaring Twenties women wore brimless cloches and asymmetrical chapeaux. During the Great Depression and WWII hats became utilitarian and somber. Veils, wide brims, and frivolity reappeared after the war. In the 1960s women copied Jackie Kennedy's penchant for pillboxes.

When women entered the workforce in larger and larger numbers, hats become smaller and smaller, eventually becoming a mere net to cover the head when in church. Soon hats were extinct, replaced by the baseball caps that men began to wear everywhere!

Women today wear a hat to protect their skin or advertise the team they play for. The milliners of the past are forgotten and their hats have become relics that surface now and then in an attic or antique shop or on the head of that rare woman of today who wears a chapeau and turns a head or two when she strolls by!

The size and style of the hats displayed in this photograph of the interior of Mrs. Henry's millinery shop, the women's apparel, and the gas lights date this image to about the turn of the century.
Photograph JCHS Collection

One of the author's favorite photographs, even though the subject is unknown! The hat is typical of those worn during the first decade of the 20th century.
Photographer Frederick E. Knapp
Courtesy Brookville Heritage Trust

Teachers from throughout the county came to Brookville for an annual teachers' institute, staying in local hotels, taking classes, and being entertained. These four Brookville teachers wore the latest in millinery when they posed for the photographer during the 1906-1907 school year. McAninch, Moore, and Mitchell taught at the high school. Emma Eisenman was later married Dr. A. McNeil. Hats became larger and larger, reaching a peak about 1911.

Photograph JCHS Collection

THE SEAT OF JUSTICE
1830

What would it be like, in the event of a summons, to saddle a horse, ride for several hours, and then make arrangements for lodging before going to court? That's exactly what folks had to do more than 150 years ago. Today even if you live in Timblin or Brockway, you are less than thirty minutes driving time of the county seat where the legal business of Jefferson County is conducted. That wasn't the case for the early settlers.

When William Penn charted his Quaker colony in 1681 and built the "city of brotherly life" that area was Philadelphia County. Bucks and Chester counties existed, too. Then through a series of treaties and land purchases, Penn's colony increased in size. The next to last purchase happened in 1768 following the end of the French and Indian war when the Six Nations assembled at Fort Stanwix. For ten thousand pounds, they granted almost all of what is now Pennsylvania to Thomas and Richard Penn. (The last small section opened Pennsylvania to Lake Erie in 1792.)

By 1785 the area now called Jefferson County was included in Northumberland County, a county that stretched across the northern part of the Commonwealth to the "Donation Lands" in the west. In 1795, about the time Joseph Barnett, his brother, and a brother-in-law set out to look for land upon which to build a mill, part of Northumberland was renamed Lycoming, and it is from Lycoming that Jefferson County was formed in 1804.

The Legislature set the boundaries of Jefferson County as beginning "at the northeast corner of Venango county (est 1800), and thence by a due south line fifteen miles, thence a southwesterly course to Sandy Lick Creek, where Hunter's district line crosses said creek; thence south along Hunter's district line, to a point twelve miles north of the Canoe-place, on the west branch of the Susquehanna; thence by a due west line until it intersects the eastern boundary of Armstrong county (est 1800); thence north along the line of Armstrong and Venango counties...."

Locating these boundaries on a Pennsylvania map today quickly shows that the county was much larger when it was founded and much larger when commissioners met in 1829 to determine the location of the county seat.

In 1804 there was no courthouse or turnpike, so official business was conducted in Westmoreland County (est 1773). In 1806 the place for official business moved to Indiana (est 1803) making it a little more convenient for the nearly 150 citizens now living in Jefferson County. That population tripled in ten years, and by 1830 the population was over 2,000.

By then the Legislature had appointed John Mitchell (Centre), Robert Orr (Armstrong), and Alexander McCalmont (Venango) as commissioners and told them to locate and fix the site for the county seat. They met at Joseph Barnett's house in Port Barnett. His friend, Moses Knapp, had moved his mill to the confluence of the North Fork and Sandy Lick in 1799, but the area of present-day Brookville was as yet unpopulated.

The Legislature had stated "the courts of justice shall be fixed...at a distance not greater than seven miles from the center of said county which may be the most beneficial and convenient for the said county." While imbibing whiskey from Barnett's still and reviewing the bids, the commissioners probably discussed what was a "central location," where a large building could be accommodated, and which place had sufficient water and drainage for a community. Sometime in 1829 these three men determined that the place where the rivers came together would be known as Brookville, the seat of county government. In their minds, they had situated its location in the approximate center of Jefferson County according to the boundaries of 1830.

Then as the number of settlers increased, the size of Jefferson County decreased. In 1843 parts of Jefferson, McKean, and Clearfield counties were taken to form Elk County. In 1848 all of Jefferson County north of the Clarion River (known as Tionesta, Jenks, and parts of Barnett and Heath townships) became Forest County. A county that had once covered more than 1,000 square miles had shrunk to an area of 655 square miles, the size it is today.

By 1850 the county's population had reached 13,518. 1,063 people lived in Brookville.

The only other borough was Punxsutawney, a town of 400 and incorporated the previous year. Between 1860 and 1922 nine more boroughs became incorporated: Corsica (1860), Big Run (1867), Reynoldsville (1873), Worthville (1878), Brockway (1883), Summerville (1887), Falls Creek (1900), Sykesville (1907), and Timblin (1922). And for all borough and township residents, the seat of justice would remain the Jefferson County Courthouse in Brookville.

PIONEER COURTHOUSE AND JAIL, 1831

From McKnight 1917

THAT MOST ESSENTIAL COMMODITY

1830—1911

Named for the numerous "brooklets flowing from the hills," McKnight confessed in 1917, "Notwithstanding this water name and watery environment of our town, Brookville, in my boyhood and early manhood days, was very meagerly supplied with water."

Pioneer families caught rain off their roofs, and housewives bought wash water from two men who sold it by the barrel. Then sixteen years after the town was named the county seat, Judge Jared B. Evans piped water from a spring near the American House on Main Street. "The conduit pipes were bored yellow pine logs, and the plant was quite expensive; but owing to some trouble about the tannery, which stood on the spot where the American barn now stands, the water plant was destroyed."

Who holds the right to water—an age-old dilemma! Is it like air—belonging to everyone? Or like minerals in the ground—belonging to the landholder? The problem arose here almost a century ago. Who would own "the most essential commodity in the life of any community?"

When Brookville lots sold in 1830, David Henry bought one and built a tannery between where the Courthouse west wing and the S&T Bank now stand. The spring there supplied his business with water. When that first water com-

69

pany began selling water to the citizens in 1846, thus depleting his supply, he took action, picked up a shovel, and dug out the pitchpine "pipeline." In the lawsuit that followed, the court decided "water could not be legally diverted from its natural course."

As the population multiplied tenfold or more, the demand for water did, too. Finally in 1883, a private corporation of men formed the Brookville Water Company and piped water from the North Fork through a six-inch wrought-iron flange pipe that was "pure, sweet and healthful." The system included the intake, "pumping station, four storage tanks, about ten miles of pipe lines and the water plugs."

An article written by Alfred Truman in 1904 gives evidence of a Mill Street Water Company as well, however he was unable to say how it was organized and operated. His concern was about its function—the reservoir apparently was not large enough to provide adequate water to all subscribers. Those at the end ended up with just a trickle!

Brookville's Main Street had witnessed four "big fires" between 1856 and 1876 and her citizens were very concerned about fire protection. With the installation of water plugs (or hydrants) water would be available to fight fire. However, it came at a cost—$25 annually for 12 of them and $16 annually for another 12 or nearly $500 a year to be paid to the corporation. That's over $10,000 in today's monetary world.

In addition to fire protection, citizens were concerned about typhoid and other water-born diseases. In September of 1906, for example, Brookville citizens were warned to boil their water due to the low water and recent rains that washed decayed matter into the streams, "making the water very impure." Brockway, Clarion, and DuBois had all improved their water systems about this time for the same reasons, and, in addition, many communities across the country were moving towards municipal ownership.

In 1911 the equipment of the Brookville Water Works was in its third decade, so the private company made the decision to construct a new filtration plant. They also erected "a very substantial dam across the North Fork creek, about three quarters of a mile from the breast of the old Litch dam."

At the same time, local editors printed articles about the national trend to municipal ownership along with the calculation that the "boro has paid over $12,000" (about $263,000 in today's terms) over 27 years to the privately-operated Brookville Water Company for use of the 12 plugs or hydrants that had been installed for use in the event of fire.

This debate over public versus private ownership continued until the middle of 1911 when the Brookville Water Company finally agreed to sell the company to borough council at cost less 25 percent off for depreciation or for $56,000 ($1,226,000 in today's terms) plus the indebtedness for the new filtration plant or a total of $116,000 ($2,539,153 in today's terms.)

When announcing the transfer of ownership, the *Jeffersonian Democrat* editor warned, "It is now up to those who have brought this transfer of the water plant to the borough to prove that it is a good thing. We believe it was the best thing to do, but we warn the town council it has trouble ahead, and expenses will have to be watched constantly."

For nearly a century, borough council and now the Municipal Water Authority has constantly been on watch assuring all of us a safe and economical supply of that most essential commodity—water.

A private company operated the Brookville Water Works, located near the present East Main Street Bridge, between 1883 and 1911.

The Spanish-style water plant built in 1911 currently supplies water to the community, but plans are underway for modernization.
Photographer Frederick E. Knapp, Brookville
Both Courtesy Brookville Heritage Trust

A century later a new water plant opened at a cost of more than $10M.
Courtesy Alan Saunders

Charles Margiotti
Photographer Frederick E. Knapp
Courtesy Brookville Heritage Trust

BELLY UP TO THE BAR!
1830—2008

In part two of *King Henry The Sixth,* Shakespeare wrote the line, "The first thing we do, let's kill all the lawyers." You can find it inscribed on coffee mugs, posters, and other gift items. In fact, there are entire websites devoted to it! But what would our democracy be without this profession? The county seat of Brookville has seen a long list of lawyers come and go over its more than two centuries of existence as a governmental entity.

Today's lawyers go to law school after earning an undergraduate degree. That was different for much of the 19th century. Like doctors-to-be who "read" medicine by shadowing a practicing physician, lawyers become members of the bar by "reading law" or clerking under the supervision of a practicing attorney. Then after passing an examination and taking an oath, they could hang out their shingle.

Between 1804 and 1830 the court matters of the people who lived here were handled in Westmoreland and then Indiana County because Brookville was not named the county seat until 1830. Shortly before the first courthouse was completed eight lawyers were admitted to the bar by the Commonwealth for the December term of 1830: Thomas Blair of Kittanning, Thomas White of Indiana, George W. Smith of Butler, Joseph W. Smith of Clearfield, John Johnston of Clearfield, William Banks of Indiana, Robert E. Brown of Kittanning, and Hugh Brady, the only lawyer admitted who resided in Jefferson County.

Soon other lawyers living in the county were admitted: Cephas J. Dunham, Benjamin Bartholomew, C. A. Alexander, and Lewis B. Dunham. Dunham was the first law student in the county and has the distinction of being the first admitted by examination. Eventually he moved to Iowa.

Lawyers often enter the political arena or rise to judgeships. Some do both. In Jefferson County, William P. Jenks was the first judge native to the county to preside at court. President judge from 1872 to 1882, he grew up in a household of professional and law-minded men. His father was a physician and his mother was the daughter of a clergyman. Two older brothers, David Barkley and Phineas were both lawyers, as was the youngest brother, George. McKnight says George was considered "one of the brainiest lawyers of his generation." William served one term in the Pennsylvania legislature (1866-1867) and George served in the United States Congress (1875-1877), before becoming solicitor general during Cleveland's first administration.

Their sister, Mary Jenks, married Isaac G. Gordon, a lawyer from another county family with multiple lawyers. He started life in Union County as a moulder, but a disabling accident caused him to turn to law. He represented Clearfield, Elk, Jefferson, and McKean Counties in the state legislature in 1860 and 1861, then was appointed president judge of Mercer and Venango Counties. In 1873 he was elected to the Pennsylvania Supreme Court and became chief justice in 1887. Cadmus, the fourth child of Isaac and Mary Gordon, also became a lawyer.

Other lawyers and residents of the county who rose to the position of president judge are Elijah Heath Clark, John W. Reed, Charles Corbet, William Thompson Darr, Jesse C. Long, Robert Means Morris, Edwin Snyder, William L. Henry, and our current president judge, John Foradora

Other lawyers have achieved eminence in other ways. Charles Margiotti), Punxsutawney, campaigned for governor in 1934 and served as attorney general for three governors. William Jack, David Barclay, James Lisle Gillis, George P. Jenks, Alexander White, Samuel A. Craig, William Smith, and Nathan Leroy Strong all served in Congress.

Lawyers are examined and admitted to practice by the Commonwealth. They voluntarily join the county bar associations. Kate M. Scott lists 39 lawyers admitted to the bar and practicing in Jefferson County in 1888 or roughly about one lawyer for every 700 people. Today, 120 years later, there are 44 lawyers who are members of the Jefferson County Bar Association, or about one lawyer for every thousand people.

No women lawyers were members of the bar in 1888. Today there are eight including attorneys Heidi Ulrich Dennison and Sharon

Smith, who were among the first women to practice here.

As for that quote from Shakespeare, there is debate in legal circles as to its meaning. Some would claim it is actually intended as praise of the lawyer's role. Others view it clearly as a "lawyer-bashing" joke, along with other of Shakespeare's references to lawyers found in *Romeo and Juliet* and *King Lear*. A person's point of view might depend upon his or her day in court, don't you suppose?

THE UNDERGROUND RAILROAD IS NOT A SUBWAY
1832—1861

Stories abound about the tunnels that run under Brookville's Main Street and some misconstrue that these openings were part of the Underground Railroad. In reality they were probably used to deliver coal to heat the buildings or to receive stock directly into the basements. Folks often blend information from different sources or "put two and two together." Sometimes the results are plausible or true, but more often they are not.

Searching for the facts in such cases can be fun or frustrating. Searching for the facts about the Underground Railroad can be very frustrating because of its secret nature. Abolitionists who were part of the story and the fugitive slaves who used the trails to escape to freedom did not want to give away their secrets. They spoke and referred to the URR in code and did not leave much of a written record.

Here in Jefferson County, some information is recorded in Scott (1888) and McKnight (1917). Scott moved to the county about 1856. In her history she mentions 1834 when "two runaway slaves" were lodged in the county jail and "outspoken abolitionist" Elijah Heath and jailor Arad Pearsall aided in their escape. She also mentions that in the same year "two darkeys made their appearance there [Beechwoods] and remained a good part of the winter."

McKnight, born and bred in Brookville, adds more to the story by devoting a full chapter in his history to the institution of slavery, abolition, slavery in Pennsylvania, the value of slaves, and the revolutionary Negro soldiers. He also mentions several Brookville people who owned slaves between 1824 and 1840 and writes, "A report in this or any other neighborhood that kidnappers were around struck terror to the heart of every free colored man and woman. Negroes of my acquaintance in Brookville have left their shanty homes to sleep in the stables of friends when such rumors were afloat."

He is quite explicit, too, in recalling what he knew about the Underground Railroad. "We had a route, too, in this wilderness. It was not as prominent as the routes in the more populous counties of the State. I am sorry that I am unable to write a complete history of the pure, lofty, generous men and women of the northwest and in our county who worked on these roads. They were Quakers and Methodists, and the only ones that I can now recall in Jefferson county were Elijah Heath and wife, Arad Pearsall and wife, James Steadman and wife, and Rev. Christopher Fogle and his first and second wives, of Brookville [Rev. Mr. Fogle was an agent and conductor in Troy as well]; Isaac P. Carmalt and his wife, of near Clayville; James A. Minish, of Punxsutawney, and William Coon and his wife, in Clarington [now Forest Co.] Others, no doubt, were connected with the work, but the history is lost. Jefferson's route originated in Baltimore and extended via Bellefonte, Grampian Hills, Punxsutawney, Brookville, Clarington and Warren, to Lake Erie and Canada. A branch road came from Indiana, Pa. to Clayville [Punxsutawney]. At Indiana, Pa., Dr. Mitchell, James Moorhead, James Hamilton, William Banks and a few others were agents in the cause."

McKnight's references can help us locate Underground Railroad locations in and around Brookville. Heath's home on Pickering Street is a confirmed sight marked by a Pennsylvania State Historical Marker.

Fogle had tanneries in Heathville and Troy [Summerville] beginning in 1825 and later in Brookville. In fact, he bought a Brookville tannery located where the old borough building now stands from Judge Heath and his co-owner. According to McKnight, Fogle may also have harbored fugitives in "the little yellow house where Benscoter's residence now is [134 Jefferson Street]."

McKnight adds that the next stop on the way to Canada and freedom was "the house of William Coon, in Clarington, Pa. Coon would ferry the slaves over the Clarion, feed, refresh, and start them through the wilderness for Warren, and when Canada was finally reached, the poor fugitive could sing, with a broken heart at times, thinking of his wife and children yet in bonds."

So, do we think those tunnels on Main Street were part of the Underground Railroad? No. Evidence does not support that idea. Rather, we know fugitive slaves arrived at Judge Heath's home (pictured) on Pickering Street as early as

1834. Heath, along with Fogle and the others probably continued to harbor runaways at their homes and places of business until the Civil War began in 1861.

The home of Judge Elijah Heath has undergone considerable change since its origin in 1831. Some think slaves were harbored in a secret section in the west part of the cellar.
Photographer Frederick E. Knapp, Brookville
Courtesy Brookville Heritage Trust

AND WHAT DID YOU SEE, CHARLEY ANDERSON?

1835

Witness Charles Anderson could neither read nor write but he did remember what he had seen on that September Sunday in 1835. Prior to the Pittsburgh court case, he had provided written testimony and signed it with his X.

Unusual for a Sunday, the extra stage had arrived in Brookville from Franklin. The two fugitives and their captor would stay in Brookville overnight before continuing on their way south to Virginia to be returned to their owners, Thomas G. Baylor and Anna Maria Baylor, minors under the age of twenty-one years, and under the guardianship of John Yates, Esquire.

Anderson slept on a bunk in the Franklin House barroom, a hotel owned by a man named Clark and located diagonally across from the Courthouse.

Anderson was a black man known about town as "Yellow Charley." McKnight writes that he was the first person to mine coal in the county for general use. His pioneer mine was located on the Clements farm, north of town, where he had stripped the topsoil down to a vein that was about two feet thick. A "little rickety one-horse wagon" provided transportation as he peddled his coal by the peck, half-bushel, and bushel to families in town. The grand prices were twelve and a half cents or an "eleven-penny-bit" for a

83

bushel, a "fipenny-bit" for half a bushel, and three cents for a peck.

McKnight describes Anderson as a "greatly abused man," because nearly all thefts were blamed on him. Later when others entered the coal business, "Yellow Charley" changed to hauling wash water and other things.

But in 1835, Anderson was mining and selling coal and living in Clark's hotel on Main Street. When Clark heard about the fugitives, he sent Anderson to the jail with supper for the two fugitives, where he stayed to watch them eat, commenting in his testimony that they ate "but little." Then the door was locked and "Yellow Charley" left with the dishes. As he passed the jail window, a quarrelsome prisoner named Butler B. Amos reached out his hands and asked for a piece. Anderson handed him the dish, then crossed to the hotel.

Before going to bed he returned to the jail where he saw John Earheart and Arad Pearsall coming along the back alley from the stable behind Thomas Hastings' hotel. This hotel was located on the present site of the Scarlet Cord. The two came to the jail window and one of them put something into the window. Pearsall saw Anderson and asked him to go to Brady's fence to get an auger that was there, but Charley refused and again went back to the hotel.

After sleeping awhile, he got up and looked out the window and saw two men standing at the jail window. They ran to the rear and Anderson followed them. They seemed frightened and, while sounds of boring and filing came from inside the jail, made him promise not to say anything. Charley left. In the morning fugitive slaves Charles Brown and William Parker were gone.

The next year, three men stood trial in the U.S. Court Western District in Pittsburgh: Elijah Heath, James M. Steadman, and Arad Pearsall. Heath owned a good bit of property and had a home on Pickering Street. Steadman had purchased the brick Franklin House from builder Daniel Elgin in 1832, but then sold it to William Clark. Pearsall, who kept a home in Brockwayville, was the jailer. All three were charged with aiding and abetting the escape of the two fugitive slaves.

When the trial ended on May 5th, 1836, the jury cast a guilty verdict and the plaintiffs were fined $600 plus costs. Their lawyer moved for a new trial, but court records dated November 24th, 1836, show that "seven hundred forty dollars ninety two cents in full debt" were paid to U.S. Court Western District, the equivalent of $16,000 according to today's consumer price index.

Today, Charles Anderson is mentioned only in a few books of local history. His burial site goes unrecognized and no obituary has been found. His testimony helped convict three white men who aided in the escape of two fugitive slaves, yet he refused to get the auger and become an accomplice. Charles Anderson did what the law of the time required—he told what he saw. But might he have shared the feelings of Hugh Brady, another witness, who stated in his testimony, "I heard there was two Negroes hand-cuffed in the stage. I went close up and seen two Negroes taken into the outer door of the jail. They was chained together by their arms. It was damned degrading to human feelings to see human beings used that way." (Quotes taken directly from 1836 court records when the word Negro was in common use.) Or was Charles Anderson's testimony his way to get even for the previous accusations of the townspeople?

Brady continued that a man named Prime, who was both a lawyer and doctor, had taken him to one side and asked Brady if they could not devise some plan to release those Negroes. Brady thought they could when they saw Elijah Heath leaving the jail. Both knew that Heath, the associate judge, opposed slavery, but he'd stated he couldn't justify a release. Prime asked Brady if Heath would not be a good hand, and Brady replied, "No, damn him! He put me in jail once." After watching Heath walk home, Prime and Brady went round the courthouse to the back of the schoolhouse and sat down and consulted whom they could get for a third man. Brady suggested Andrew Straub could be trusted. Prime went to get a quart of whiskey and both got drunk. Neither knew anything more of the Negroes until the next morning when they heard they had escaped.

Today a Pennsylvania State Historical Marker identifies the home of abolitionist and judge Elijah Heath, 64 Pickering Street, in Brookville.

THE DEAD WRITERS SOCIETY
1837-1930

Browsing through old newspapers has been an avocation for many years. I'm married to a sports enthusiast and volunteered long ago to sit at the History Center on Sunday afternoons rather than in front of the TV. There I've become acquainted with Kate, Dr. McKnight, Alfred, "Neighbor" Kennedy, and others who took time to describe the people, places, and events of our community. Sometimes they even expressed their opinions!

Kate Scott was twenty in 1857 when her father moved from Oliver Township to Brookville and joined Samuel McElhose in publishing the *Jefferson Star.* Two years later, he founded the *Brookville Republican.* After the Civil War began, Kate volunteered and served several months in 1861—1862 as a nurse with the 105th Pennsylvania Regiment at Camp Jameson, Virginia.

Upon her return she ran the *Republican's* editorial department and was "in charge of columns." She was secretary of the 105th Regimental Association 1879—1891 and of the National Association of Army Nurses of the Civil War 1897—1911. She worked with the Grand Army of the Republic, helped establish the Pennsylvania Memorial Home, and lobbied for pension benefits for Civil War nurses.

She also documented our history. Original copies of her books in our archives include *A History of the 105th Regiment* (1877), *History of*

Jefferson County, Pennsylvania (1888), and *The National Association of Army Nurses of the Civil War* (ca 1910). We also have original issues of the *Brookville Republican* as well as other local newspapers and there are numerous references to her comings and goings. She died on April 15, 1911, and her tombstone in the "New" Brookville Cemetery reads "Army Nurse, Authoress."

We are grateful to Kate for her thorough documentation of much of our history here in Jefferson County. She compiled the facts up to 1888 in an easy accessible form, but in her books Kate did not express her opinions.

Dr. William J. McKnight copied many of those facts in his books, but he also included memoirs of events. His articles appeared in local papers, and he continued to revise his work, publishing *A Pioneer History of Jefferson County, Pennsylvania: 1755–1844* in 1898, *Pioneer Outline History of Northwestern Pennsylvania* in 1905, and finally, his two volume *Jefferson County, Pennsylvania: Her Pioneers and Her People* in 1917.

Included in the first of two volumes are his personal recollections of Brookville between 1840 and 1843, sitting in church, his involvement with and opinions about the Southerland exhumation in 1857, and the need for appropriate legislation concerning the dead. When I find one of McKnight's recollections interspersed among his documentation, it makes for interesting reading. While facts are certainly important, it's fascinating to learn what he thought and felt about people, places and events.

A favorite of mine is his recall of fun when he was a boy in 1840:

> We boys amused ourselves in the winter months by catching rabbits in box traps, the woods were full of them, skating on Geer's pond, a small lake then located where Algeier's brewery now stands (this lake was destroyed by the building of Mabon's millrace), skating on Barr's (now Litch's) dam, and coasting down the town on graveyard hill. In the summer and fall months the amusements were alley-ball behind the courthouse, town-ball, over-ball, sock-ball, fishing in the streams and in Geer's pond, riding floats of slabs on the creek, swimming in the 'deep hole,' and gathering blackberries, crabapples, wild plums, and black and yellow haws. But the amusement of all amusements, the one that was enjoyed every day in the year by the boys, was the cutting of firewood.

Imagine that, boys enjoyed work! Or is McKnight adding a touch of sarcasm here? Also note where these amusements took place and the four kinds of ball games they played. It's these little details that help us see these boys at play here in our town.

Alfred Truman didn't write a book; instead he wrote "hundreds of descriptive pieces concerning his travels for the press as well as discussion on matters of leading interest." He was sixteen in 1861 when he arrived from Nottingham, England. An engineer, he worked with Wright and Callen on the design of the first logging railroad in Pennsylvania and later vividly described the first run of the train near Callen Run in 1864. His numerous columns published in local papers cover a variety of events and people. A longtime friend and admirer of the extended Bowdish family, he wrote about them several times, expressing opinions about their genius and ingenuity. He, too, recorded details. It is his writing that helps us know the kinds of amusing rides that Albert Neal Bowdish and his two older boys built when Charles was just a toddler.

Another local writer, Richard M. Matson, wrote a forty-three page paper titled "Biography of R. M. Matson by himself," a title I find amusing! His autobiography relates his growing up, school, farm life, his brief law career, timber ventures, public service and politics, and finally his retirement in Florida. I enjoy reading and learn much from these topics, but as the mother of three, I find Matson's stories of his youth especially interesting. For example, he writes:

> We all attended church, with the exception of one person that stayed at home to keep the house. Once I prevailed on them to let me stay and keep the house. The family had not gone long until the lonesomeness and quietness of the place began to tell on me and I looked around for something to do. Finally I discovered the powder horn. I took it down from the nail on which it always hung and made a long streak of powder the entire length of the front porch about 30 feet in length. When all was ready I obtained a live coal from the fireplace and touched off the train. It went off all right but left a streak as black as ink the entire length of the porch. I had plenty to do from that on trying to obliterate the damaging evidence of my folly. The result was not as satisfactory as I wished, and when the

family came home the porch was wet and the black streak was still there. Grandfather scolded a little but Aunt Jane and Grandmother did not say much and I no doubt kept as still as possible, while they enjoyed my embarrassment. One was enough. I never asked to keep house on Sunday again."

Matson's book The *Story of the Christ As Told by the Evangelists* was printed in 1916.

Another writer concerned with religious topics was Ira C. Fuller, a Brookville entrepreneur who operated several flour mills and was involved in banking before opening his own banking house in 1881. It later became the National Bank of Brookville. His close friend, Alfred Truman, described him as a man who had read, observed, and traveled, and who used his "versatile brain" to become "a man of world-wide conception and information."

Fuller was born in 1828 and in his later years he became acquainted with the spiritualism movement. A strong group in the last half of the 19th century, spiritualists anticipated the dawn of a "New Age" or period of utopian and religious social reform. In fact, the spiritualist newspaper printed in Boston was called *The New Era*. The editor believed that angels were the spirits of deceased humans. Pamphlets, tracts, directories, and handbills were printed, too, but most have not been preserved.

Spiritualism is a historical phenomenon and was closely tied with the progressive or radical intellectual, political, cultural, and artistic movements of the time. The Chautauqua programs evolved during this period, and so did Lily Dale, a community built in 1879 in upstate New York. Today Lily Dale is the world's largest center for the spiritual development and practice of the Spiritualist religion.

During this time Brookville hosted an annual "Chautauqua," or series of intellectual programs that were offered in a tent. Ira Fuller most likely enjoyed stretching his intellectual capacities at such events. It is quite possible, too, that he may have traveled to Lily Dale to hear the lectures, meet best-selling authors, participate in workshops, learn the latest in scientific research into psychic phenomena, and become acquainted with mediums and healers.

Truman wrote, "...while in the region of religion his whole thoughts carried him to the loftiest heights of metaphysical research." Fuller's inquiries into metaphysics during the later years of his life led to the writing of four books: *Romance of Jude, Romance of the East, Poems and Essays,* and *Tutelary Gods and Ancient Spirits.* They all pertain to the spirit world.

Writers of history, memoir, and even metaphysics help us step back in time. By reading their writings of almost a century ago and by examining the world in which they lived, we can understand the changes their world was undergoing and try to understand better the changes our world is undergoing today.

Kate M. Scott
1827-1911
Sketch by Mima Haverty

William J. McKnight
Frederick L. Knapp
Photographer
Courtesy
Brookville Heritage Trust

Richard McConnell
Matson
Frederick E. Knapp,
Photographer
Courtesy Brookville
Heritage Trust

24/7 SERVICE AT THE PUMP
ANN AMELIA CLARKE
1843—1917

Service round the clock seven days a week isn't simply a phenomenon of today. More than a century ago, one woman thought drinking water should be available no matter the day nor hour a person or horse became thirsty. Her idea, a lighted fountain on Main Street, became a reality on October 24, 1903.

On that occasion county historian William J. McKnight ended his dedicatory address, saying, "...by authority of the Brookville Village Improvement Association, and in the name of virtue, equality and temperance, I christen this, our public drinking fountain, *Harriet-Amelia*." The good doctor was referring to Harriet Burns, president of the Association, and Amelia Clarke, who must have inherited her concern for the community's well being from her father.

Her father's obituary described him as "one of its most worthy and respected citizens, earnest in everything that tended to the good of the town. He was for a number of years one of the overseers of the poor, and in him the unfortunate and needy ever found a friend."

When Clarke died in 1883, the property transferred to Amelia, her sister, and her husband. Later they deeded their share to her. Eventually declared legally blind, Amelia lived there until her death in 1917. Between 1971 and

95

2004, the building functioned as the Jefferson County History Museum.

Along with food, clothing, and shelter we humans need water. McKnight and historian Sherman Day both give accounts of Brookville's water supply. In 1843 Day wrote, "The place now contains about 50 or 60 dwellings and stores, a large brick court-house and public offices, and a Presbyterian Church. The town is watered by hydrants, supplied by a copious spring in the hill on the north." In 1917 McKnight recalled, "Notwithstanding this water name [Brookville] and watery environment of our town, Brookville in my boyhood and early manhood days, was very meagerly supplied with water. That which the people had and obtained from deep and expensive wells was, as a rule, disagreeable in taste and of an inferior quality."

He continues by describing the organization of the Brookville Water Company in 1846. The company routed the water "through logs buried in the ground, just as it naturally flowed. The logs were laid down Jefferson to Pickering, down Pickering to South side of Main Street, and west from Pickering on Main to Barnett." This system, however, did not last. The next attempt at providing water did not happen until 1883 when water from the North Fork was piped through wrought-iron flange pipe.

According to an interesting deed recorded in 1871, that spring utilized in 1846 was located near the Clarke property. The deed permits the property owners living on the south side of Jefferson Street "the right to attach a water pipe of sufficient capacity to supply the house and lot...." The owner of these water rights had the right to enter the other property to make repairs and to "carry a sufficient amount of water to her lot aforesaid for the necessary, ordinary and useful purposes thereof forever, but not to allow it to continuously flow...." Living near this "copious spring" Amelia must have taken part in discussions about water and water rights.

In 1898 she did extensive remodeling in the house that may have been built as early as the 1840s but most certainly by the 1850s. She added typical late 19th century door and window moldings, fireplace mantels, and faux finishes to much of the woodwork. Faux or false wood graining is a technique that developed in 17th century Europe when slow-growing hardwoods became very expensive. Wood finishers instead used special tools, paints, and glazes on the faster-growing softwoods like pine and poplar to simulate the grain of hardwoods like oak, walnut, and bird's-eye maple.

About the same time Amelia was remodeling her home, several people on Main Street had had their homes wired for electric lights, and soon electric streetlights replaced the gas lamps. Amelia must have put two and two together because in 1901 she began to work on her idea to have a lighted fountain in front of the courthouse. She gathered the women of the Village Improvement Association together. To raise the more than the $900 needed, they held tea parties in her home and sponsored other fund-raising events. And a lighted fountain was built!

97

Amelia Clark died in 1917. In her death as in life, she was charitable, leaving large sums to individuals as well as the Brookville Cemetery Association, the Philadelphia Home for Aged and Infirm Blind Women, and the Pennsylvania Institution for the Instruction of the Blind. We have yet to track what became of *Harriet-Amelia*. We do know, though, that the town constable was ordered to maintain her!

The line was long as horses awaited a drink at Amelia Clarke's lighted water fountain, or town pump as it was sometimes called, in front of the Jefferson County Courthouse about 1903.   Photographer Frederick E. Knapp.
Courtesy Brookville Heritage Trust

WHAT'S IN A BUILDING?

1845—2008

When I was a National History Day coach, a team of students began their project by identifying a building and saying, "We want to tell the story of the house my parents lived in when they were first married." In their research, they discovered that the vice-president of the United States had dined there prior to the government's decision to enter the First World War. Those young students learned a lot about American history as they prepared to tell the story of a house.

What can we learn about American history by studying the building the Jefferson County History Center lives in? People often ask us about the expansive Nathan Greene Edelblute Building, named for the person who built it. When the Jefferson County Historical Society (JCHS) undertook its preservation and adaptation as the Jefferson County History Center in 2001, we were committed to preserving as much of its 19th century character as we could. And so when one proceeds through the History Century Shop into the rest of the building, the grand walnut staircase and frosted transom embellished with NGE are there to behold.

In the E. M. Parker Gallery on the first floor the wonderful arched windows look out onto the new patio. Upstairs the full shutters for most windows remain as do five fireplaces and their mantels. Wide baseboards, elegant single and double doors, and some of the original lighting fixtures remain, too. Truly, the Nathan Greene Edelblute Building is one of the jewels of Brookville's Historic District.

These architectural features confirm the wealth of the builder, but don't tell us how he became wealthy or why he chose to live in Brookville. We do know that Nathan was ten in 1847 when his family left Blair County and arrived in Clarion County. They were on their way to Kansas, part of that group of "westward ho" Americans. He became a merchant at the age of 13 and when his family left for Kansas in 1855, he moved to Brookville.

A set of letters dated 1855, addressed to Nathan and found in the older section of the History Center (northeast quarter of the building), include a list the nineteen-year-old made on New Year's Day 1856. He listed 6 pairs of pants (1 good), 4 vests, 5 coats (1 good), and 6 fine shirts. He wrote that he had clerked for men named Amived (sic) and R. Arthurs, and had run logs on the Clarion River. His income for that year—$215.

One county history explains that "the Nathan Green Edelblute dry goods, clothing, notions, etc. commenced business in 1859," but doesn't provide a location. Nevertheless, by 1860 we know Nathan's parents had moved west and he had taken a wife, Rosetta Frank, a daughter of Brookville businessman David Frank, and they were parents of a 1-month-old son named John.

The enterprising clerk now had his own business. By 1874 he had a farm as well and was raising, selling, and racing trotters. One of four deadly fires swept through Brookville's Main Street area in 1874, and Nathan took that opportunity to buy Fryer's property (where the west part of the History Center stands.) He proceeded to build the large west retail store, the front east retail area, and the large apartment on the second floor where his family would live. These new parts surrounded the northeast quarter of the present building built in the 1840s or 1850s.

We think the family entered their living quarters through the large double doors in the middle of the building and proceeded to the lower parlor (the present research room) and kitchen (small archives). They reached the second floor by climbing the grand staircase or the back staircase off the kitchen. The formal parlor, ballroom, and four bedrooms were on the second floor.

The Edelblutes raised their family there. The marriage of daughter Ada to Elmer Pearsall in 1890 took place in the parlor, and Nathan moved to Punxsutawney the next year. After Elmer left for reasons unknown, Ada remained in the family residence until her death in 1946.

After Nathan moved to Punxsutawney, the large retail space that had been the N. G. Edelblute Dry Goods Store (pictured in *Caldwell's Atlas* in 1877), housed in succession, Patterson's Drugstore, Trautman Drugs, Western Auto, and the DuBois Courier office. The smaller east retail space housed a billiard parlor, Lena

Jackson's millinery shop, Guth's Jewelry, the Pel Shoe Store, and the Carousel Gift Shop. After Ada's death the heirs used the residence area to store family furnishings.

And what does this building tell us about American history? Nathan Greene Edelblute was an enterprising young American who used his business acumen to take advantage of post-Civil War economic opportunities. This was a period of rapid economic growth and a period when people sought luxury goods. Edelblute capitalized on that good fortune.

Nathan and Rosetta Edelblute posed with family members in a studio sometime around 1890.   *JCHS Collection*

RISK TAKER AND TIMBER ENTREPRENEUR

RICHARD M^CCONNELL "MAC" MATSON

1845—1930

His great-grandparents, Uriah and Belle Matson, came to Indiana County from Ireland. Their daughter, his Aunt Susan, met Moses Knapp when he attended school in Indiana. They married and settled on the banks of the North Fork. John Matson, Uriah's son and Susan's brother, brought his wife to a farm in Rose Township in 1805. They raised ten of their own children in addition to their grandson, Richard McConnell, whose mother, Minerva Reynolds Matson, had died when he was quite young.

Richard's father, Uriah (the second so-named) acquired extensive lumber holdings, and when the boy was fifteen, allowed him to pilot his first raft alone. In his autobiography written during the last decade of his life, Richard wrote,

> I was very fond of the water and would take chances that I now know were dangerous. Father was rafting below town and sent me up the creek to turn loose a stick of timber he wanted. The men were to catch it when it floated down to where they were working. I concluded there was no use me walking back those two miles, when I could ride. So I pushed the stick out into the stream and perched myself on top. A more frightened set of men you never saw than they were when they saw me riding on that log. Everybody got ready and as I sailed by several pike poles were fastened into the timber

and I was pulled to the shore. Father seemed to be somewhat out of temper, but I could see no reason for so much fuss about a little matter like that."

Too young and too small to enlist, Richard went to work in his father's store during the Civil War and received business training that was "a very valuable asset" to him during his lifetime. In the spring of 1865 he went to work for W.H.M'Laughlin in Pittsburgh measuring timber and keeping the books. Returning to Brookville, he read law and taught a short time in the Steele School, a job he disliked.

He passed the bar and married in 1866, but discovered finding clients in a town with some of "the best lawyers of the state" was difficult, so he partnered with W.H.M'Laughlin and started a store that became successful. Over the next seventeen years he tried law again, opened and closed another store, lost money in a sewing machine deal, dabbled in politics where he usually lost, and ran a raft or two of shingles and such to Pittsburgh. Richard McConnell Matson was not afraid to venture forth, to lose, to succeed, and to learn from his experiences.

Finally at the age of thirty-eight, he and four others purchased timber and a saw mill in Forest County. He wrote that the mill business was not doing well but that he was determined "to stay until the job was finished," and moved his family to Forest County for the summer. He later concluded, "Here I laid the foundation for a knowledge of the lumber business that has been of great use as I have continued in the sawmill business up to the present time.... I look back on the time spent in the woods as the most pleasant part of my life. My family were all at home and were working on the mill and we thoroughly enjoyed life."

In 1895 Matson and Levi Heidrick bought interests in the Litch holdings on the North Fork, and the two of them were the active managers until 1898 when they sold out to Cook & Graham, "making the mistake of our lives." The price of lumber rose and Cook & Graham made money.

By the turn of the century much of Jefferson County's timber had been cut and timbermen looked west. Matson and Heidrick purchased tracts in Wisconsin, West Virginia, and Alabama. Yet this Matson kept his home in Brookville, spending the last years of his life overseeing these interests and traveling during the winters with his second wife.

For the most part, his three sons, Uriah Jullian (the third so-named in the Matson family), George R., and Norman D. remained in Jefferson County, carrying on the Matson lumbering tradition.

Richard Matson built this American "foursquare" home at 102 Main Street in 1903. Pictured on the front porch are a woman and two boys, possibly his second wife and two grandsons.

Photographer Frederick E. Knapp
Courtesy Brookville Heritage Trust

ALBERT BAUR AND THE BANJO
1846—1920

Curiosity leads people to collect things, and when a collection assumes a critical mass, some think of creating a museum. Thus, we have museums that exhibit nothing but bicycles, toasters, or postmarks.

Manufacturers sometimes devote a section of their factory to an exhibit of the products they've designed and produced over time. In Bradford, you can visit the Zippo factory museum where 15,000 square feet of lighters and other things are on display. In DesPlaines, IL, you can see the re-creation of McDonald's #1 along with other McDonald's memorabilia.

Universities build museums on their campuses. At Penn State you can visit the Palmer Museum of Art, the HUB-Robeson Gallery, and the Pattee Library where even a Paterno Retrospective exhibit was once on exhibit!

In 1973 the University of South Dakota established the National Music Museum in Vermilion and among their collections are banjo journals, original manuscripts, photographs, and a personal scrapbook with Brookville connections. Years ago Mr. and Mrs. Thomas Scribner Canning, who lived in Morgantown, WV, at the time, donated this collection, all of which were connected in one way or another to Albert Baur, who lived in Brookville between 1865 and 1920 when he died.

107

Baur was born in Reading and grew up in New York City. He fought with the Hawkins Zouaves and the 102nd Light Infantry, NY Volunteers, in the Civil War, marched with Sherman, and lost a leg at the battle of Kenesaw Mountain in Georgia. He made his way to Brookville in 1865 to clerk in the American Hotel that was managed by his uncle, Charles Kretz. A decade later, he married the manager's daughter and they had a son. Baur was in charge of the Western Union Telegraph Company for 16 years, then tried real estate in Flushing, New York, between 1883 and 1885. It was there, in New York that his fame grew.

Prior to the American Revolution, African slaves, who were forbidden to play drums, had developed a primitive form of banjo. Fretless, with three or four strings, this instrument was fashioned from a calabash gourd, and covered with a hog skin, goatskin, or sometimes the skin of a cat. They used whatever was available for the strings—horsehair, gut, twine, or hemp. The banjo created by these Africans lacked respectability and was considered to be lowlier than the fiddle. The banjo was an instrument that the "good folks" knew was from the devil.

But in the early 1800s, black men on the family farm taught a white boy named Joe Sweeney to play that unrespectable instrument. By 1845, he'd organized a minstrel troupe, and the instrument became an overnight sensation. Joe Sweeney died before the Civil War began but his brother, Sam, entertained the headquarters staff in the Army of Northern Virginia, and the

108

enjoyment of banjo music spread rapidly among the troops. Today, when we think of the Forty Niners, minstrel shows, Stephen Foster, cowboys, Appalachian Mountain hollows, and the halls of Harvard and Yale, the lively music of the 5-string banjo comes to mind.

Using a quote located on the Internet, we might surmise Baur used a popular instruction book during the Civil War. "A very good idea of the old style of playing may be formed by referring to 'Briggs Banjo Instructor'" wrote Albert Baur, Sgt., Co. A, 102nd NY Volunteer Infantry (To our knowledge, Tom Briggs is not in our family line!) Baur's obituary tells us he'd studied music for many years and "especially the playing of the banjo." By the time he moved to Flushing, he had a reputation. He played before audiences in large cities on the coast, became nationally known, and Europeans knew of him as well. During his lifetime he arranged and composed over 3000 pieces of music.

Sometime after 1885 he and Susan began furnishing the Longview Hotel, a venture that historian Kate M. Scott deemed successful, but his obituary claimed that "he was such a strict landlord that he lost heavily on his venture." Later they lived at 135 White Street and he operated a grocery store on Main Street. In 1890 he was elected Justice of the Peace

Jimmy Canning lived on Main Street and he, too, ran a grocery store. Baur taught Canning to play the banjo and eventually they recruited other members and formed the Brookville Banjo, Mandolin, and Guitar Society.

Banjo music continued in popularity through the end of the 19th century when phonographs became popular and the importance of live music performances dwindled.

Today the American Banjo Fraternity is one non-profit organization that keeps the music of the 5-stringed banjo alive. Local readers may find it interesting that the group holds fall meetings at the Pantall Hotel in Punxsutawney and they are acquainted with Brookville's Albert Baur! (www.abf.org)

A sketch drawn by James Canning includes Al Baur on the left.   Sketch donation of Ruby Canning.

SLEUTHING FOR CLUES
1850—1946

At the History Center it is not uncommon for a newcomer to come in with a question about the house they've just purchased. Sometimes we have a file that will help. Other times we point the way to courthouse records.

The History Center is no different than those new homeowners. When we became owners of the Nathan Greene Edelblute Building in 2001, we were anxious to find the clues that would help us learn about this elegant 19th century building.

From tax records and written histories we know, for example, that around 1830 William Rodgers opened a store in a room "on the lot now owned by Nathan Green Edelblute. We know that in 1845 J. G. Clark began the "erection of [a] large brick storehouse on the site now occupied by the Edelblute Block." We know, too, that his son William kept a store there for more than twenty years, while living elsewhere. In 1853 a document from the assessor's office shows his "dwelling and stable" as lot #117, and his "storehouse and office" as lot #66, later identified as Edelblute's lot.

The best clue, though, is found in Scott's 1888 history, where she writes that William Clark built an addition in 1850—and provides the dimensions! It didn't take us long to use our tape measure and discover the dimensions of the office and gallery B match Scott's! The northeast section of the History Center is indeed the addition built by Clark in 1850.

Next, to learn about Nathan himself, we looked at census records, a brief biography, and a genealogy. His family moved from Blair County to Clarion in 1847, and then to Manhattan, Kansas, in 1855. At age 13 Nathan entered the mercantile business in Clarion. When his parents moved on, he moved to Brookville, and by 1859 he was dealing in "dry goods, clothing, notions, etc." The 1860 Census lists 22-year-old clerk Nathan G. Edelblute, his 18-year-old wife Rosetta Frank, and a 1-month-old son John. Rosetta was the daughter of David Frank, an early Brookville business owner and perhaps the man who owned the Globe Hotel in 1856-57. It was located where the Scarlet Cord now stands. Might Nathan have stayed there when he moved to Brookville? Might Rosetta have set eyes on him there? Or had they met when both the Franks and the Edelblutes lived in Clarion? We do not know.

While county records and history books are good sources, papers found in a building are even better. One day in 2002 our general contractor called to say workmen had found a crate of papers in the crawlspace above the northeast or older quarter of the building. Donning rubber gloves, then sorting through rat-infested newspapers and such, we discovered letters written to Nathan in 1855. On New Year's Day 1856 when he was 18, he listed his worldly goods and his income for the year: 6 pairs of pants (1 good), 4 vests, 5 coats (1 good), and 6 fine shirts. He had clerked for a man in Clarion and for Richard Arthurs in Brookville, and run logs on the Clarion River—all for the grand annual sum of $215 (the equivalent of $5524 in 2008).

So what do these clues tell us about the building the History Center now inhabits? We know Rodgers and the Clark father and son had a store or stores on the property almost from Brookville's founding in 1830. We know Nathan Greene Edelblute arrived in September 1855 from Clarion. We surmise he might have clerked or lived in the northeast quarter of the present building because that is where letters to him were found.

During the next 15 years he married, operated his store, and established the Red Bank Stock Barns that were located on the fairgrounds near the rivers where he raised, raced, and sold trotters. We know that the 1874 fire destroyed Fryer's building to the west, and that Edelblute was wealthy enough by then to buy that lot and begin construction of the present building that wraps around the older building (the northeast quarter) that was already there.

Edelblute operated his dry goods store on the west side of the building. Lena Frank Jackson, his sister-in-law had her millinery shop on the east side. The family entered their residence through the large double doors in the center and either went to the rear of the building (the older section) where there was a parlor and kitchen or up the elegant staircase to the second floor where the ballroom, parlor, and five bedrooms were located. A stone stairway, stable, and out-house were located at the rear of the property.

In 1890 Nathan's daughter Ada married Elmer Pearsall in the upstairs parlor. Two hundred guests attended. Nathan ran his store until 1891, then moved to Punxsutawney and operated a store there. Patterson's Drug Store, Trautman Drugs, Western Auto, and the DuBois Courier subsequently occupied the west side. A billiard parlor, several millinery shops, Guth's Jewelry, Pel's Shoe Store, and the Carousel Gift Shop occupied the east side.

Ada continued to live in the family residence until her death in 1946, dying according to Pearsall heirs in the room now termed Gallery A!

THE VISUAL ARTISTS AMONG US
1852-1951

We do not know who cut the intricate tombstones that dot the many cemeteries of Jefferson County. We do not know the stencilers whose murals decorate the grand ballrooms. We do not know the 19th century portrait painters because, as a rule, nineteenth century artists in Jefferson County remain anonymous. Most artists of the twentieth century did sign their work, and for that, those of us who keep track of such things are grateful.

A recent JCHS acquisition is a watercolor titled *Poppies* painted and signed by artist Margaret Craig. We know just a little about her. Born in Brookville in 1852, she moved to Washington D.C. where she died in 1951 at the age of 99. We don't know of other paintings by her and she is not listed in any of the sources we reviewed, however, her obituary claims she was "an artist of note."

Unlike the art of southwestern Pennsylvania that is documented in two books edited by Paul A. Chew, art in our area has not been documented. The Jefferson County History Center would like to remedy that gap in our history.

Thanks to his daughter, one visual artist whose work is documented in detail is painter Elmer William Youmans who grew up in Reynoldsville. The sixth of seven children, he was born in 1919. His aunt, Francisca Doolittle

Snyder, lived with the family and was the artist who became his inspiration.

During his high school years Youmans filled many roles for the *Reynoldsville Star* newspaper, including artist. He attended the Phoenix Art Institute in New York, and studied under Franklin Booth, Norman Rockwell, and others. During WWII, he served as an army artist and camouflage instructor in the United States, Iceland, England, and France. Between 1964 and 1981, he was a staff artist for the Pennsylvania Historical and Museum Commission.

Primarily an oil painter, Youman's work has been exhibited in Johnstown, at Indiana University of Pennsylvania, at the PA Military Museum (Boalsburg), as well as the State Museum in Harrisburg. Youmans died in 1991 and is buried in a Reynoldsville cemetery. Fortunately, his daughter, Kathy Youmans Duvall, has the portfolio or photographic record of his work and the information about where most of his paintings are.

In 2003 the History Center hosted a series of workshops about the arts in Jefferson County. Participants listed visual artists and photographers they remembered or who were mentioned in books and newspapers, or who are living today and either live here or paint scenes of the county. Names mentioned include Anna Barclay, Anthony Bonnett, Charles Bowdish, Nancy Byers, Nell Clarke, Margaret Craig, Carl Crouse, Edwie Clauser, George Fryer, an artist named Hurd, Frederick Knapp, "Beanie" Lucas, Mary North, Charles Park, Adam Sabatose, Emma

Slick, the wife of a Dr. Scott, Bert States, and the father and son photographers named White.

Living artists and photographers include Doris Bickle, Anthony E. Cook, Mary Lynne DeKiep, Nevin Delacour, Joe Enterline, Dennis Faber, Joanne Garrett, Ray Garvey, Jeanne Green, Jean Guthrie, Deena Greenberg, Mary Hamilton, Dorothy Hook, Kevin Kaltenbaugh, Arnold Knape, a woman named Lavender, Brian McManigle, Daniel Miller, Dick Pasi, Jo Rickard, Mandi Crain Stein, William Stein, David Strohm, Bruce Sykes, Geneve Thrush, and Joe Young. We suspect this is only a partial list of the visual artists and photographers that create today or who have created and left their work behind.

The arts can be defined as either fine or folk, terms not related to the quality of the art but dependent upon the professional training of the artist. The art of Elmer Youmans, by virtue of his training at the Phoenix Art Institute, is considered to be fine art as is the work of Punxsutawney artist Joanne Garrett who studied at the Philadelphia Academy of Art. Grandma Moses, the painter of dear New England scenes, had no professional training, yet her work hangs in museums the world over. Her work is considered folk art.

Be it fine art or folk art, at the History Center, its documentation is important because art is part of our cultural heritage. The art we create is part of what makes us who and what we are. That -is why we encourage artists here in the county to create a digital record of their work if possible, or to simply make a list of the work, when it was created, and where it is now, and to bring a copy to the History Center for the archives. If you know of artwork created in or about Jefferson County, let the History Center know about it. Working together we can document our creative past.

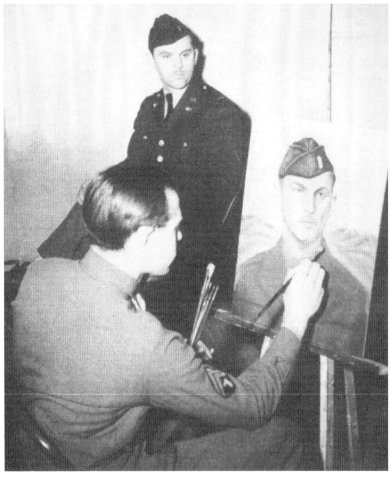

Professional painter Elmer Youmans did portraits when serving in Iceland during World War II.
                              Courtesy Kathy Youmans Duvall

UNIQUE TO THIS PLACE
1854—1901

Most folks enjoy bragging a bit about being first or best or biggest! Yet here in Jefferson County few know that the county was first in two important innovations that improved the production of timber and boards and helped boost the county's economic development.

The early timber men were limited to where they could cut timber because once a tree was felled, it had to be dragged to a mill. So trees were felled on hillsides that sloped toward the many streams that meandered through the region. The men could then use a sledge (a tool with runners) or horses or oxen to move logs to the stream. In the winter they would build a slide and keep it iced for sliding logs down the hillsides.

In those early days rafting was limited also by the low rivers and streams. Water high enough to move logs or the raft platforms only happened two to four times a year. When high water was imminent even the editor of the local paper joined in the work, announcing the following week why no paper had been printed!

Then Thomas K. Litch arrived in town from Pittsburgh where he had been a successful inventor for his company located at the "Point." Litch is credited with inventing the "Clipper," the engine that powered steamboats on the Ohio and Mississippi rivers and building the first hand fire-engine used in Pittsburgh. He'd moved

119

from Massachusetts to Pittsburgh and in 1850 saw opportunity in the timberlands of the north and moved his family to Brookville.

He also recognized that the streams in the county needed maintenance much as our roads of today do, so he and others formed the Red Bank Navigation Company in 1854. The company maintained the waterway between Brookville and the Allegheny; more specifically, the state legislature granted them the power "to clean and clear the Red Bank, Sandy Lick, and North Fork from all rocks, bars, and other obstructions; to erect dams and locks; to bracket and regulate all dams now erected; to regulate the schutes [sic] of dams; to control the waters for purposes of navigation; to levy tolls not exceeding one and one-quarter cents for each and every five miles of improved creek, per thousand feet of boards or other sawed stuff, for every fifty feet, linear measure, of square or other timber."

"To bracket and regulate all dams..." a key phrase that leads to an innovation credited to Jefferson County by historian Benjamin Kline. The bracket dam is a way of creating an artificial flood that can move logs downstream during times of low water. Whether it was Litch and the Redbank Navigation Company that came up with the idea or whether local timber men were using the system when Litch arrived is unknown. What is known is that the system worked.

The bracket dam had two parts, an earthen and wood reinforced dam to hold back the water, and a sluiceway, lined with planks on both sides and on the bottom. When the water behind the dams reached a certain height, the brackets were cut at the point along the stream where the first rafts were to be floated. This continued along the tributaries until the artificial floods reached Brookville. Each person responsible for cutting the brackets was notified by telegraph or handbill, as to the exact time when to cut the brackets and how many.

The second important innovation credited to Jefferson County was the logging railroad of Wright and Pier. They purchased land on Callen Run in 1863 and soon built a mill. Wright thought up a way to use a locomotive instead of horses to draw logs over his tramroad. He consulted with a fellow named "Brush" Baxter and the two of them traveled to Pittsburgh to buy a small portable boiler and engine. Alfred Truman recalled later that he and Silas Miller of Brookville were the only engineers in the area, and that he, Alfred, was all of eighteen! Nevertheless, Miller and Truman converted the boiler and engine into a locomotive.

Invitations were issued to attend the first run of "The Little Wonder," an event that demonstrated its ability to move along the wooden rails and up and down the grades. Soon the Little Wonder was busy transporting logs to the mill. And so was Alfred Truman who was invited to run the train all alone, including loading and unloading it! "The laborious work of loading the car alone was not the only difficulty to contend with, but added to that was the work scrambling from the engine to the log car, over the logs to brake on coming to the various steep pitches, and then back to the engine again."

So the next time talk turns to timber, feel free to brag a little!

T. K. Litch designed a series of dams on the North Fork making possible artificial flooding that would send logs and raft platforms downstream. Evidence strongly suggests this type of dam originated in Jefferson County.
Photographer Frederick E. Knapp
Donation of Rose Blake Ames, Brookville

More than 150 years after its invention, a replica of the Little Wonder is used during special days at Cook Forest State Park.   Photograph courtesy HerbA

Lewis Earle Sandt was not the only risk-taker of his day. Sam Scribner took a financial risk in New York City when he and his partner established the "Columbia Wheel."
Photographer unknown, JCHS Collection

FROM TUBA PLAYER TO TYCOON
SAMUEL ALEXANDER SCRIBNER
1859—1942

Dr. McKnight knew Sam Scribner and described him as "decisive in speech, rough and ready in action, unalterable and uncompromising in honesty and fairness." Scribner is remembered here as the poet who named two hundred townspeople in his poem "To Ellis," recorded by Garrison Keillor for the Jefferson County Historical Society several years ago, and as the dynamo who organized a memorable Brookville event in 1920. Many are unaware of his life as a show business tycoon in New York City and the impact he made upon the American entertainment scene.

In 1920 hometown boy Samuel Alexander Scribner turned 61 and returned from New York City to provide the impetus and "pep" for a committee of sixty people who represented townships and boroughs and who carried out a grand Old Home Week in conjunction with the 1920 fair. Local newspapers claimed "no better booster than Sam Scribner can be found in the country." Yet his early days in Brookville had not been without trouble and turmoil.

Scribner was born on August 18, 1859, in Howe, Eldred Township, just north of the Brookville town limits, to Alexander S. and Cynthia Scribner. He had a brother and sister. After his parents divorced, his father remarried and Sam found himself with four half-siblings.

The musically talented Scribner went to school, but was a somewhat rebellious student. He apprenticed to a blacksmith at seventeen and ran away within the year to play the tuba in a circus brass band. He led the circus life for nearly two decades before forming the All New Enormous United Shows, a traveling circus, with partner Neil Smith. By 1902 Barnum and Bailey had bought it, and Scribner, with a new business partner, John Herbert Mack, had founded the Columbia Amusement Company.

The significance of the Columbia Amusement Company or the "Columbia Wheel" to performers cannot be underestimated. By coordinating bookings in 38 theaters east of the Mississippi, Scribner and Mack changed the fly-by-night existence of thousands of burlesque and vaudeville entertainers and provided work for them in a systematic way throughout much of the year. Burlesque acts would form a troupe and travel together from city to city during all but the summer months, and Scribner and Mack would become wealthy. By 1923 the property value of theaters owned by the Columbia Wheel exceeded $20 million.

According to a New York Star press release, "Columbia Burlesque is one great system of entertainment so closely knit that its general manager, Sam A. Scribner, sits at his desk in New York...controls the destinies...and supervises the duties of nearly 3,500 people during eight months of the year. And in the course of a season more than $5,000,000 slide into the pay envelopes of Columbia employees."

Scribner's importance to the life of American entertainment is well documented by Carolyn Martin in the 2004 *Bronxville Journal*. "The spirit of men such as Sam Scribner lives on ..., men who carve their own way with energy, vision and persistence. Scribner was given almost nothing except his own strength of mind and character, his playful humor, his vitality and generosity, but he fashioned these qualities into a remarkable life. He began in dim obscurity, fueled by his charismatic persona, and lit by the glare from the Great White Way, his star reached extraordinary heights."

But was Scribner really given "almost nothing"? Or during his early years in Brookville did he rub up against people who were examples of strong mind and character, who were humorous and playful, and who possessed vitality and generosity? Whatever Scribner gained from his early years, it is obvious that he never forgot his Brookville roots for he returned often, choosing to ignore the troubles and turmoil of his youth.

He had returned often enough during the forty-five years he'd lived in New York to be able to call upon a large number of friends in 1920 to carry out plans for the Old Home Week. He did his part, too, promoting it in theaters where his shows were booked. Scribner and the others organized a full week of special events including a massive Education Day, an Old Timers Ball Game, an Industrial and Labor Parade, an air show, and a band concert. Brookville hotel rooms were full, tents and cots were called for, and people were asked to open their homes.

Between September 12 and 18, local reporters estimated more than 50,000 people visited the fair and the Old Homecoming events making the week an unqualified success. Sam Scribner may have in the Bronx most of his life but he remained a Brookville boy at heart. When he and his wife Etta died in the early 1940s they were both buried in the Brookville Cemetery.

AWAITING COLLEGE
CYRUS H. BLOOD
1860—1913

Helen Darr Briggs hated her middle name—Blood—a name she acquired because her parents were friends with the Blood family. Brookville folks are familiar with the three-story brick Parker P. Blood Building (est 1875-76) that now houses the Area Agency of Aging and Penn State Cooperative Extension offices.

Blood roots go back to 1833 when Parker's father, Colonel Cyrus Blood, a mathematics professor at Hagarstown Academy, purchased 6000 acres where Marienville stands today, naming the town after his daughter. He was active politically as an associate judge and county commissioner, and instrumental in forming Forest County in 1848. His sons, Kennedy L. and Parker P., became active businessmen and politicos in Brookville, Kennedy representing Jefferson, Elk, Clarion, and Forest counties in the Pennsylvania State Senate about the time the Civil War began.

Kennedy's son, Cyrus H., turned seventeen in 1877. He had begun keeping a diary earlier but unfortunately the History Center has only volume two in its collections. Nevertheless, his entries tell us a good bit about daily life for a young man of his time. We can imagine him on Main Street, clerking in his father's store, perhaps doing the same in his uncle's drugstore in the new Parker P. Blood Building, and making daily visits to a local newsstand so he could follow the burgeoning baseball league, the war in Europe, and politics in the United States. Cyrus was very systematic about listing daily scores in his diary and the pertinent war news

He refers to many political events and to his father's term of office in the State Senate, as well as his trip to Philadelphia for the Democratic State Convention in 1877. He also refers to the death of Wm. Erdice on September 3, 1877. "Mr. Wm. Erdice, an old & prominent citizen of this place, died today at 11 o'clock A.M. Age 68 years. He had been sick for the first time. Although I do not wish to bear any malice towards the dead, I cannot but remember that this is the man who first handed over to the hands of the Sheriff our property for sale. He having seized the store & had it sold. He might have permitted Father to have continued the store & he would have gotten his money in time. But then it is done and cannot be undone & so let it be."

Cyrus aspired to go to college. He'd graduated from grade eight and may have taken classes at local academies. (Brookville's first high school class did not graduate until 1886.) But by reading between the lines of his diary and referring to several other sources hints reveal that the family finances may not have been in good shape and that his fall plans were "iffy."

"I think it all together likely that I shall go to the Washington & Lee University, Lexington, Virginia, this fall & take the 2 or 3 year course & then if Father is able to send me, go to Princeton. This is my programme now."

To prepare himself, he made arrangements for Dr. George Means and Father Weinker at the Roman Catholic Church to tutor him in Latin. His diary records his progress.

His father and the Presbyterian minister, Reverend Cummins, had established a drugstore in 1850. Parker P. replaced Cummins several years later and the two brothers operated the store until 1870. Then the 1874 great fire destroyed the building.

Cyrus (pictured at age 13) writes in September, "Did very little today. Expect to go out to Forest Co. In the morning to see how the oil well is prospering," a clue that his father and uncle were perhaps speculators in the recent western Pennsylvania oil boom.

Finally, he mentions his father's trip to Philadelphia, perhaps for treatment on "his limb." *Caldwell's Atlas* published in 1878 also refers to his father's "precarious" health. This series of events—the sheriff's sale, a serious fire, oil speculations, and poor health—may have resulted in poor family finances for the Kennedy L. Blood family in 1877, in spite of the fact that K. L. owned 1425 acres in Rose Township.

Nevertheless, someone recognized that Cyrus had potential for in September he writes, "After all I expect to go off to school on next Monday. Mr. H. R. Fullerton of Parker City has kindly offered to advance the money & I am to pay it back In time. I think I shall go to either Lexington, Va. Or Meadville, Pa. Hipla — Hoopla — Good bye Brookville for 6 or 8 months."

131

Cyrus H. Blood did indeed go on to higher education attending Washington and Lee University in Lexington, Virginia. He then read law with Jenks and Clark in Brookville and was admitted to the bar in 1883. On June 3, 1885, he married Maude Darr, sister of William T. Darr, a lawyer and father of my mother-in-law, hence her name—Helen Blood Darr.

At a young age, Cyrus H. Blood became enamored with the new game of baseball.

JCHC Collection

SOME GAVE THEIR LIVES
THOMAS REYNOLDS M^CCULLOUGH
1863

He bears two important names in Jefferson County. The McCullough family was one of the first families to homestead in Pinecreek Township. The Reynolds family gave their name to Reynoldsville. Cemetery tombstones chiseled with McCullough and Reynolds are silent memorials to these families in both places, but no stone bears the name Thomas Reynolds McCullough.

His family settled here and began to clear the land so they could farm. Thomas may have attended one of the early schools organized in the county, or perhaps it was his mother or father who taught him to read and write. For write, he did.

When President Lincoln called for new soldiers in the spring of 1863, Thomas signed on and became a member of Company I, 148th Regiment of Pennsylvania Volunteers, Colonel Peale's Brigade, Hancock's Division. The company trained and then moved to southern Virginia.

Thomas purchased a small diary and began to describe where he was, what the weather was like, and what he and his fellow soldiers were about. What follows are selected entries from his diary. Some spellings and punctuation have been modified, but the context remains as he wrote it.

133

"April the 28th, 1863—Our regiment marched up the river four miles and encamped there for that day then there was 150 detailed for picket duty.

"April 30th—We started to march to the river; we marched two miles toward the river, then we halted and took dinner. Then about 4pm, we started on our march for the Rappahannock River, and we crossed on the pontoons about dark, and we marched upon the flat and rested then we started...and we passed one of 150 of rebel skirmishers, and we marched five miles south of the river.

"Sunday May 3rd—This morning, the firing commenced again and continued till about 2 o'clock when the line on the right of us gave way and let the rebels in our rear, and they poured the shells into us from two or three different ways. We thought it was our own men, and they sent word to them to silence that battery, for they were shelling our own men, and they found it was the rebels, and they had us almost surrounded, and there was an order came long the line to sling knapsacks and close in on the left, and the rebels was so close on our rear, that they took eight of Company K prisoners, and then we retreated to where the rest of the regiment was laying behind the breastworks, and that evening, there was some heavy cannonading done and after roll call, we lay down to sleep, and we was wakened up twice by heavy musketry. On the left for a few moments then nothing more was heard that night.

"Wednesday the 6th—This morning, we crossed the river, and the mud was knee-deep and marched back to our old camp with our pants all mud and our guns red with rust.

"Sunday May the 11th—Preaching today in camp by the chaplain prayer meeting this evening at dusk by our chaplain, and not very many to attend the meeting.

"Monday May the 12th—Clear and warm this morning; rumors of moving today this evening. Governor Curtin is in camp this E. and the brass band was heard all over camp.

"May the 17th—Warm, out this morning, and I am carrying water two [sic] wash my clothes, and I had to fall in rank before I got through with my washing.

"May the 27th—Cloudy and cold, nothing going on in camp and today. I washed a shirt.

"May the 28th—Warm and clear today. There is a service at half past eight o'clock by General Hancock. And this day nine months ago, I was in Brookville.

"Sunday June the 7th, 1863—Cloudy and cold. Our men are crossing the river on the pontoons at the left of Fredericksburg, and our men still continue shelling the rebels.

"Sunday June the 14—Cloudy and cool, and we are packing our knapsacks for a move, and W. M. White died this morning, 18 years. And on Sunday evening, we started on our march, and marched pretty near all night.

"June the 20th—Cloudy and cool and at 12 o'clock, we started on our march again, and we marched over the Bull Run battleground and on to Gainesville and through hay market and from there, to Thorofare Gap and being very tired, we made our beds without getting any sleep or supper.

"June the 27th—Today we stayed in camp till 4 o'clock and marched to Foolsville and on through Barnesville and about a mile.

"June the 29th—This morning, we renewed our march at 7 o'clock and marched around Frederick City and through another small town and then marched through a town called Liberty and marched a little further and through another small village and through Johnstown and marched until night and halted and rested, and then started again and marched through Uniontown and encamped a little ways from the town...

"June the 30th—Cloudy and warm this morning, and we have muster, for pay today, and there is a big detail for picket today."

A bullet pierced the diary during the battle at Gettysburg, and Thomas Reynolds McCullough was buried somewhere nearby. Today he is among those listed at Gettysburg as having given their lives.

GETTYSBURG AND THE 105th
1863

If you were one of the many who watched Ken Burns' heart-breaking television program, "The War," you know the bond established among those who fought. They shared an experience most of us cannot begin to fathom.

Civil War veterans bonded following that war, too. Here in Jefferson County, men returned, some to resume the livelihood they left, others to adapt because of injury, and some to be buried, but it did not take long for those who fought to create an organization that provided opportunities to reminisce about their shared experiences.

The Grand Army of the Republic, or GAR., was organized in 1866 in Illinois, to "preserve kind and fraternal feelings;" to assist former comrades, widows and orphans; and "to maintain allegiance to the United States." Post No. 134 organized in Brookville on June 25, 1868, lapsed between 1878 and 1882, was then reconstituted as Post No. 242, also known as the Captain E. R. Brady Post. Punxsutawney, Reynoldsville, Brockwayville (now Brockway), Corsica, and Sprankle Mills also had GAR posts. In 1888, county historian Kate M. Scott noted there were 6,000 posts nationally with more than 300,000 members.

These groups held local and joint meetings as well as statewide and national encampments. Upon the 50th anniversary of the Battle of Gettysburg, 45,000 veterans, including more than 100 from Jefferson County, returned to Gettysburg. Among them were Captain S. A. Craig (105th), W. H. Gray (105th), and W. J. McKnight (57th Mil.) The majority "enjoyed the great gathering to the full, although some became discouraged with the uncomfortable conditions existing early in the encampment and returned home."

For Pennsylvanians Gettysburg does come to mind when the Civil War is mentioned, but Gettysburg, like every community, has a history of change over time. The land that became Adams County supported Native American people. Europeans arrived. Settlers farmed and congregated in villages. Two sides met and fought. Then what?

> The stench alone was overpowering. Even five miles away it was sickening. Great clouds of flies were equally loathsome. They hovered over the trampled crops, rocky woods, and blasted fields. They drifted over the litter of hats, coats, blankets, haversacks, diaries, love leters, Bibles, daguerreotypes, rifles, swords, and empty cartridge boxes to settle on the putrefying carcasses of perhaps 5,000 horses and over 7,000 young men rotting in the summer sun.
>
> Mark Jenkins for
> National Geographic News 2003

As time passes, how does a community change? The clean-up—memorializing—commercialization—and now the restoration are all part of the changes in that particular place named Gettysburg. Granted—a very famous place!

Here we did not have to clean up a battle-field, nor deal with the commercialization and restoration of a national site. Our citizens did, however, bury the dead and memorialize the event. More than a year before the Battle of Gettysburg, a group of men gathered intent upon forming a new cemetery north of town. Surely, they must have had in mind the need to care appropriately for the town's dead soldiers. They purchased 14 acres from Uriah Matson and oversaw its clearing and beautification. Workers built roads, walks, an entrance gate, and a caretaker's house.

Then as bodies arrived, they were buried in the new cemetery, small stones marking each grave, but there was no monument. Community-minded Paul Darling, a bachelor, died in 1881. He left large sums to many institutions and individuals and two thousand dollars for a monument, a "handsome granite shaft" of 32 feet, topped by a life-size figure of a private at "parade rest." The Grand Army of Jefferson County dedicated it on May 26, 1885.

The following year the local GAR. joined the memorialization of the battlefield itself. Officers of the Monumental Association of the 105th included O. C. Redick, S. A. Craig, J. C. Kelso, K. M. Scott, and W. H. Gray. They raised funds, visited Gettysburg, and selected the field to the right of the Emmettsburg road, "where the regiment did its hardest fighting." The monument to the "Wild Cat Regiment" was finally dedicated on September 11, 1889. Scott and a relative were there.

139

On November 19th, 1863, Abraham Lincoln had memorialized the dead at Gettysburg by saying:

> It is rather for us to be here dedicated to the great task remaining before us—that from these honored dead we take increased devotion to that cause for which they gave the last full measure of devotion—that we here highly resolve that these dead shall not have died in vain—that this nation, under God, shall have a new birth of freedom—and that government of the people, by the people, for the people, shall not perish from the earth.

Yes, we do memorialize the dead with monuments and memories—and with a recommitment to government of, by, and for the people.

We memorialize our veterans locally, statewide, and nationally. Those still living in 1923 are pictured above for the rededication of the soldier's monument in Brookville. First dedicated in 1918, a fourth bronze panel was added on July 1, a day declared as "All Soldiers' Day."
Photographer Frederick E. Knapp, Brookville
Courtesy Brookville Heritage Trust

OLD MACDONALD HAD A FARM
1869

A century ago more than two thousand farms dotted h county and the greater percentage of our rolling hills were planted with crops and grazed by dairy cattle. Today that is not so. Much of our land has returned to forest. More significantly, the number of people who claim to be full-time farmers has dwindled. Only half of the 548 farms of today are farmed by full-time farmers.

Kate Scott described the farms of 1888, "Farms that in former years scarce yielded a pittance, have not been brought to a high state of cultivation. The unsightly stumps are all disappearing; good fences have been built, while the best and most approved farming implements an machinery are in general use. On the farms the log cabin, and the rude stable have given place to the large well-appointed dwellings, and commodious barns....Within the last few years a great interest is being taken in the improvement of stock, and now some of the very best grades are to be found in this county, until it has become noted abroad for the fine horses and cattle raised and owned by our stockmen....Jefferson county is also becoming noted as a fruit-producing region, the soil and climate being especially adapted to the raising of almost all kinds of fruit except the peach....Apples, pears, cherries, grapes, etc., are grown in the greatest profusion and perfection."

Nathan Greene Edelblute, the man who built the building that houses the Jefferson County History Center, was one of the first to turn to raising horses. He'd earned his living in dry goods in the early years of his marriage, then began raising trotters in 1869. His Red Bank Stock Barns held about forty horses in the area that is now the Memorial Park between the rivers. He raced his horses in several states.

Another farmer W. H. Gray, introduced Guernseys into the county, bringing in two heifers and a bull from Chester County. By 1936 large dairy farms predominated. After World War II, with one cow for every four county citizens, the value of dairy farming in the county was estimated at $1M. In 1958 the local newspaper reported that 8,400 cows were milked each day, yielding more than 60 million pounds of milk for the year. Potatoes and peas were important cash crops.

During the Great Depression, many farmers had been forced to turn to other work and gradually over the last half of the 20th century the number of farmers and farmers decreased. By 2002 the 2,567 farms and 154,636 acres of farmland of 1880 were reduced to 548 farms and 86,899 acres. However, thanks to improved farming methods, each acre earned about 33% more.

Jefferson County is home to some farms that have remained in the same family for more than a century. In 1988 Jean Harriger documented 46 of them in a small book, *The Century Farms of Jefferson County, Pennsylvania*. She included the original acquisition of the land she lived on, ownership changes over time, and finally the repurchasing by various family members, an illustration of how historical events and physical attachment to "place" impact land ownership and use.

Solomon Heriger purchased 145 acres in Knox Township in 1853, and when his four sons became adults, Joseph D. received 44 acres. He in turn gave 27 acres to his son, William H., whose son, Russell or "Hap purchased the 27 acres in 1963 Russell and his wife, Jean, then bought an additional 75 acres that was in the original 145 acres and other family members purchased other parcels. Not called Hariger Hollow, the original 145 acres have grown to about 1,1000 acres owned by Solmon Heriger's descendants.

Fewer than one hundred acres remain cleared. No longer farmed, the rest has returned to forest and used for hunting. The Jefferson County Longrifles lease six acres of the Russell Harriger property for their club headquarters and shooting facilities. Of an interesting note, this leased land is the same land Solomon Heriger purchased in 1853.

Half of those 548 farms are farmed by full-time farmers, and a handful of them are larger than 500 acres. Any of the others do what is termed "niche" farming, agriculture aimed at specific markets and often farming that is tied to the increasing awareness of consumers. These farmers show up at local farm markets or make weekly deliveries to "pick-up locations" where people get a week's supply of fresh produce and other products. Or they raise speciality crops like blueberries, Christmas trees, maple syrup, honey, herbs, pumpkins, or animals like alpacas!

Jefferson County farmers, like farmers all over the country, have adjusted over the years to the demands of the consumer and to the pressures of the marketplace. In today's world of increasing energy costs, local farmers will continue to do that.

Mules stop for a rest on Brookville's Main Street. They are being transported to Broadacres where they will work the land for the Reitzes, whose forbearers arrived in Jefferson County in 1842 and who, in addition to Broadacres, farmed The Highlands, Johns Farm, Miller Farm, Reitz Haven, and Cloverdale. Today descendant Harry Reitz owns and operates Cloverdale just south of Brookville on SR36.
Photographer Frederick E. Knapp
Courtesy Brookville Heritage Trust

VERSATILITY WITH THE CAMERA LENS

FREDERICK E. KNAPP

1869—1948

Imagine a hot and humid July or August day. Graduation has come and gone. Portraits are finished and paid for. June weddings are over. The photographer paces up and down in his second-floor studio across from the courthouse and mutters to himself, "What next?"

Then, he pauses at the window, looks west to the American Hotel, then east towards Harrison Matson's building across from the Courthouse and Markle's Market where an orderly stack of melons sits near the curb. Dancing down the steps and through the door, he crosses Main Street, chats a bit with a friend on the corner, crosses Pickering, buys a melon, and totes it back to his studio. Then over the next hour or two, he devours the melon, and takes a set of photographs of himself doing so!

I was fortunate to see this set of self-portraits many years ago when here at the History Center we began to identify photographs taken by Brookville photographer Frederick E. Knapp. Relatives brought in the framed set for me to see and I was immediately taken by this humorous fellow that I never knew.

Another self-portrait that we do have in our collection shows him attired in ragged

145

clothes, an old slouch hat, and a false beard. He has a twinkle in his eye and is playing a violin.

We've processed many of Fred Knapp's photographs over the years—formal portraits of local businessmen, buildings around town, railroad sidings, automobile wrecks, hunters with their kill, and even glamour shots of local young women—all taken between 1898 and 1945.

He was indeed a versatile inquisitive photographer with a sense of humor. Born in Pinecreek Township in 1869, he was the great-grandson of Moses Knapp, Brookville's first settler of European descent. Fred went to the local schools, then farmed and did stone masonry until 1890 when he went to work in the studio of photographer E. C. Hall.

More than a thousand years ago people knew how to use a pinhole camera to produce an optical upside-down image. Someone published information about this process in 1600 and men like Vermeer, the artist featured in the film *The Girl With the Pearl Earring*, used it to assist with accuracy as they painted. Daguerrotypes appeared shortly before the Civil War, followed by other processes like calotypes, ambrotypes, ferrotypes, and glass plates. Then in 1884 George Eastman invented the film process that predominated during much of the 20th century.

Knapp grew up with these changes in photography. Hall most likely taught him to use a large view camera and glass plates, but Knapp recognized there was more to learn about the process of making pictures and went to Pittsburgh for eighteen months to study and gain experience. When he returned from Pittsburgh he bought the studio of J. S. Vasbinder.

Historians Scott and McKnight cite a long line of his predecessors, photographers like Witman & Cobb (1850), Simeon Snyder (1851), Bridge (1853), Chase (1853), Marlin (1854), Windsor(1857), Dillon & Abram Hall (1858), Fuller (1859), Harry Darr (1861), E. Clark Hall (1862), W. H. Gray (1866), Hall & Gray (1875), Wilt Bros (nd), Hoffman (1876), and again E. Clark Hall (1875). They don't mention Vasbinder, however his 1942 obituary tells us he was "a lifelong resident and photographer."

In his new studio and for the major part of his career Frederick Knapp used a view camera and glass plates. The History Center, through a partnership with Historic Brookville, Inc. cares for a collection of about 700 of them. Their rescue is a story in itself. Following Knapp's death in 1945, the studio was cleared out and much of his work transported to the town dump. Editor H. E. "Pud" McMurray heard what was happening, recognized their historical significance, and rescued as many of the glass plates as he could. For many years they were stored at the offices of the *Jeffersonian Democrat*.

During the 1990s, editor McMurray's sons, Don and Bruce, approached Historic Brookville, Inc. and the History Center about the preservation of Knapp's glass plate negatives. They now are owned jointly through the Brookville Heritage Trust and have been preserved and documented at the History Center through a grant from the Pennsylvania Historical and Museum Commission. Today visitors can use the computers at the History Center to view digitized images of Knapp's photographs.

Photographer Frederick E. Knapp had a wonderful sense of humor, illustrated here in a self-portrait (above). Was he also playing tricks in the image below?
Photographer Frederick E. Knapp
Courtesy Brookville Heritage Trust

THE SHACK CALLED BLUEBIRD BUNGALOW

GEORGE WASHINGTON HEBER

1872–1936

Ephemera and *provenance* were unfamiliar words to me when I first delved into the curatorial world. A colleague explained that ephemera are all those things, particularly paper things that last for only a limited time—like the program from a class play or a circus poster. Here today, gone tomorrow unless someone tucks one away. Provenance means origin or source or where things began. When folks come into the History Center with a possible donation or loan, one question asked is about provenance. Did this thing have its origins in Jefferson County? What is its connection to this place?

If curators cannot establish a connection, they sometimes suggest where the right home might be. Periodically, too, curators review collections and sometimes find things that should be returned to their place of origin.

Recently a large scrapbook of clippings and ephemera found its way from the Swedenborg Museum at Bryn Mawr, Pennsylvania, back to Jefferson County. The album had begun its life in 1925 when George W. Heber built an addition onto the two-room "shack" on Clark Street that his uncle, George Heber, Sr., had built at the turn of the century.

149

The scrapbook ends with the signatures of three relatives from Springfield, PA, on August 6, 1963. One took the time to write, "The cottage began as a two-story two-room shack on two acres of ground owned by his uncle, George Heber, Sr., in the early days of this century. George W. lived at the family homestead beside North Fork Creek at the bridge [the house no longer stands.] He loved nature and farming and quiet. These he found at the 'shack.' There were no neighbors, no streets—nothing but the sounds of nature. He explained his liking for the spot because he said, 'Every man should have one place as his own, where he could stand on his hind legs and tell the whole world to go to hell.' It became a family tradition when entering the grounds of the cottage to get out of whatever conveyance took them there, turn away from the cottage, and raise the thumb to the nose. Aunt Kate Heber called it the Indian salute. When the grounds and shack were inherited by George W. Heber, he turned it into a beautiful spot that was visited over the years by others as well as the family. With the death of George W. Heber the 'will to survive' began to depart from the cottage."

George W. Heber was a bachelor with multiple interests—radio, music, entertaining, birds, horticulture, and history. He collected things. Organist at Holy Trinity Episcopal Church for 47 years, he added to Bluebird Bungalow in 1925, where he entertained often. Nearly 2500 signatures are recorded in the scrapbook—names of local people and the names of musicians who were guests at luncheons, musicales, recitals, and garden parties.

Heber had studied music under Walter Hall, a famous English organist, and his wife, a noted pianist. He also studied the mandolin under Valentine Abt. According to present-day string players, Abt (1873-1933) was one of the greatest of the early American mandolin soloists. His compositions were published, and he also made a handful of recordings, for example his *Artist's Valse,* for the Victor Talking Machine. Heber was a member of the Brookville Mandolin, Banjo, and Guitar Society.

Heber earned his living as the proprietor of the Brookville Musical Headquarters and was secretary and general manager of the Solar Electric Company and general manager of the Brookville Water Company. He was a key member of many community organizations and projects. As secretary and general manager of the Brookville Cemetery Association, he compiled and printed the rules and regulations and organized annual "flower days" at the cemetery. He arranged for trees to be planted on the hospital grounds to honor pioneer doctors and Civil War nurses.

Pertinent to the Jefferson County Historical Society is the chartering and incorporation of the George W. Heber Historical Society of Jefferson County, a process he began in 1927. Heber was known for his collection of historical objects and exhibited them in 1930 when Brookville celebrated its centennial as the county seat. The present JCHS owns the charter and therefore, we were pleased to find Heber's typescript and edited draft of the original by-laws tucked within the pages of this album.

Mention is made in the scrapbook that Heber "has written a history of Brookville and vicinity." To the best of our knowledge, no known copy exists today.

When the Presbyterian Church building of 1870 was torn

MUSIC ROOM, GEORGE W. HEBER, BROOKVILLE, PENNA.

down in 1904, the organ went into storage until George W. Heber bought it in 1925. He installed it in the new wing he had added to his father's "shack" on Clark Street. During the next ten years, several thousand people visited the"Bluebird Bungalow" for luncheons, musicales, and evening entertainments.

Postcard
JCHS Collection

GUESS WHO'S COMING TO BROOKVILLE?

1872

Rochester police arrested Susan B. Anthony on November 5, 1872. Anthony was charged with casting an illegal ballot and jailed. Fifteen other women joined her in this transgression of voting laws in New York.

Susan B. Anthony had a long history as a proponent of civil rights. She argued for the abolition of slavery, admission of women to the professions, equal pay, an eight-hour workday, limiting the sale of liquor, dress reform, property rights, and child custody rights for women, but she is remembered most for her fight for woman's suffrage.

Anthony had organized a convention in 1848 in Seneca Falls, New York, where she first promoted her declaration for women to the group of men and women assembled there. Both she and her close friend, Elizabeth Cady Stanton, wrote and spoke on behalf of woman's suffrage and other issues. Even though Anthony didn't rate herself highly as a speaker, she became part of what is known as the American lyceum.

The lyceum idea had emerged in America in the early part of the 19th century as a way to provide common knowledge and ideas for the expanding American population. Community groups in the northeast and midwest promoted these debates and forums for lecturing. In small towns like Brookville, committees of local folks sponsored visiting lecturers like Anthony.

The *New York Tribune* named Anthony, along with Frederick Douglass, William Lloyd Garrison, Wendell Philips, Antoinette Brown, James Russell Lowell, Herman Melville, and others in a list of 202 individuals available for the 1859-1860 series. After the Civil War, these lyceum lectures became a commercial enterprise and a way for celebrities and others to expand their incomes. They were paid between $75 and $150 for each lecture ($1500-$3000 today).

Between January 1868 and May 1870 Anthony had written and published a newspaper called *The Revolution.* Circulation grew to 3000 but after twenty-nine months she realized the newspaper was not paying for itself, and so publication ceased, leaving her with a large debt. She again turned to the lyceum as a way to earn something when she wasn't tending to her duties as an officer of the National Woman's Suffrage Association (NWSA) and signed on with the Redpath Lyceum Bureau, which had offices in Boston and Chicago. Their list of lecturers for the early 1870s included many reform-minded persons like Anthony.

We know from biographies that on May 11 and 12 of 1871 she attended the annual meeting of the NWSA in New York City, then returned to her home in Rochester, New York. Within a week or two, she left Rochester to meet Stanton in Chicago, and we suspect that she detoured to

Brookville in order to fulfill a lecture commitment.

The Brookville Lecture Committee had advertised that Miss Susan B. Anthony, "The Great Champion of Female Suffrage," would lecture on June 2nd. Indeed, she did arrive by stagecoach and spoke in Nicholson Hall, a building that stood almost across from the History Center. General admission was fifty cents and reserved seats seventy-five. The weather had turned quite warm reducing attendance a bit. Nevertheless the newspaper's next issue reported that the Friday evening event had been well attended and that her two and one-half hour lecture, "Power of the Ballot," was well received.

Later that year Anthony and Abigail Scott Dunaway traveled more than 2,000 miles in the American northwest where she spoke in hundreds of churches and halls on behalf of woman's suffrage.

It was the following year, 1872, when she and fifteen others decided to demonstrate in a very visible way their commitment to achieve suffrage for women in the United States. Anthony stood trial but refused to pay the fine of $100 that was levied. Suffrage for women was finally achieved in 1920, sadly too late for Susan B. Anthony who had died in 1906.

Sadly, too, Nicholson Hall no longer stands on Main Street. The third of Brookville's great fires raged between Pickering Street and Franklin Avenue and burned the entirety of the south side of Main Street on the 20th of November

ber 1874, as well as much of the area west of the History Center.

In 1920 Elizabeth Marlin McCreight became the first Jefferson County woman to cast a vote in a federal election, seventy-two years after Susan B. Anthony began her quest to secure the vote for women. To her right (in front of curtain) is Cleveland Endres. Fred Sayer wears glasses and is at the end of table. Out of the camera's range is Mrs. William T. (Hope) Darr who was prepared to serve tea at this momentous event. However, she was overruled by Judge Corbet.

Photographer Frederick E. Knapp, Brookville
JCHS Collection

"THE GO" OF BASEBALL IN BROOKVILLE

1877

Cyrus H. Blood played baseball the afternoon of his seventeenth birthday before escorting Ada Dickey "to the Ice Cream Saloon" where they refreshed their palates "with that cooling dish." During that summer of 1877 he recorded in his diary his own involvement in local games as well as the scores of various games played across the country. Occasionally he mentioned Ada.

He didn't differentiate among National League teams, International Association minor teams, or various college teams. All were baseball—a game on the go! Cartwright standardized the rules in 1845, and during the Civil War, young men introduced the game to others. When it took off after the war, young Cyrus H. Blood, born May 26, 1860, took off with it!

He liked the Alleghenies, the minor team that became the Pittsburgh Pirates, and recorded the scores of other minors like the Tecumsehs, Buckeyes, and Rochester. He included teams from Amherst, Harvard, Rutgers, Weslyan, and Yale, and followed the Athletics, Boston, Chicago, Cincinnati, Hartford, Louisville, New York, and St. Louis—all eight teams of the two-year old National League.

The game was so new, in fact, that its spelling was not yet standardized. Cyrus refers

157

to *ball, Base Ball, base ball, Alley ball, BaseBall, alley ball,* and *baseball*! Local newspapers of the time use both Base Ball and base ball. The first local reference we located was in 1866, when "the Base Ball Clubs" played their daily game near the White Street Bridge. The next year a 4th of July game between "married and single gentlemen" resulted in "an easy victory to the married party."

Cyrus grew up with the game and on June 1, 1877, after recording a tie game between Allegheny and Indianapolis wrote, "13 innings were played when the game was drawn. A base ball tournament is to take place at Genesee, N.Y. beginning July 2. $1000 purse money is offered."

Might that "purse money" have inspired him to organize a "tournament" between Brookville and Reynoldsville. He writes, "We go up to Reynoldsville next Wednesday & feel pretty confident of winning." The game was 4th of July entertainment for both communities. He adds later, "Today a greater part of Brookville went up to Reynoldsville. I have very little to say. The baseball match came off and we were beaten most terribly. Score Reynoldsville 23. Brookville 8. Our boys played very losely [sic] at the close of the game we held them level until about the 6th inning & then our boys give way. They will probably return the game now."

Cyrus practiced daily and team spirit was high before the return match three days later. "If we don't give them one good beating, it will be because we don't know how. I feel pretty confident of winning as do the rest of the boys. It was perfectly outrageous that we permitted them to win.... We will never be so foolish again....I think if we are beaten I will quit playing ball."

Cyrus blamed the umpire for the Saturday loss. "The Reynoldsville Club came down today & contrary to all expectations we were again defeated but by a very close score. We won the game however fairly & squarely, but as there was a good deal of money staked, the umpire was very unfair. We 'kicked' [complained] several times & made him reverse his decision. This excuse may appear very lame, but it is actually the case. Another thing that beat us partly was that none of us could catch. Graham's underhand throwing & a good many balls passed. The score stood: Reynoldsville 19. Brookville 17."

The *Brookville Republican* writer, however, saw the game a bit differently, "The playing was rather wild on both sides, but the Brookville boys seemed to labor under the greatest difficulties, their pitcher sending the ball to bat with such force that the catcher could not take them, thus allowing their opponents to take numerous bases on passed balls; they also discovered that a successful game cannot be played without some practice, which they have not had."

In spite of his threat to quit playing, Cyrus did not. "....We sent wording to the Reynoldsville B.B.C. that we were ready to receive a challenge from them to play for $50 aside & all the outside bets they wished....BaseBall has been at fine heat....BaseBall never had 'the go' so before—in this place at least."

159

Baseball, indeed, had "the go" in Brookville! It continues to this day when teams of people of all ages play America's favorite pastime in our communities. As for Cyrus, he continued to play pick-up baseball during his college days in Virginia. And Ada Dickey, the girl he treated to ice cream? Well, she faded from the scene and he married Maud Darr in 1885!

This Brookville team played around the turn of the century evidently well enough to want their photograph taken by a professional photographer!

JCHS Collection

"CLIFF" DEEMER'S ORISKANY BUG

1878—1959

Following Drake's 1859 discovery but nearly two decades before the birth of Frank Clifton Deemer, the riverboat Venango transported fifty barrels of oil to Pittsburgh—and started the oil boom in northwestern Pennsylvania. Eventually the Standard Oil man visited Jefferson County searching for more black gold. During this search for oil, natural gas was discovered, and by 1887 the Jefferson Heat and Light Company was piping it from Knox Township to heat Brookville homes.

People have known about oil and natural gas for hundreds of years, but it wasn't until 1885 when Bunsen figured out a way to mix natural gas and air to create a flame that many of today's uses began to evolve. Pipelines did not become numerous until the 1920s, so its use by the Jefferson Heat and Light Company in 1887 was unique.

During these years "Cliff" was growing up in Emerickville where his father was a blacksmith. When his father, Alexander D. Deemer, opened a dry goods store in Brookville, the family moved into town. "Cliff" attended Brookville High School where he played football. Following graduation, he attended Grove City College and Duff's Iron City Business College in Pittsburgh before going to work running the Bell Mill for his early to young Deemer. When only seven, his fa-

161

ther had encouraged him to understand the world of business by giving him an interest in a gas well at Iowa Station. By the age of twenty young "Cliff" had drilled and sold interests in a successful well along the Clarion River. He'd also invested in the stock market as a young teen only to be wiped out in the panic of 1893 leaving him $7500 in debt. His problem at the turn of the century—how to liquidate that debt?

When his father organized the Deemer Furniture Company in 1901, "Cliff" recognized the company as a potential buyer of natural gas, along with the new Twyford Motocar Company, and the Brookville Glass and Tile Factory, three young industries located in the southeast of Brookville. Later he boasted he'd started his business on a two-cent stamp when he mailed a letter to Katherine Bell Lewis in Buffalo and asked if he could market the gas from her well in Knox Township.

By 1910 when commenting on the birth of his first son, the local editor described Deemer as "the proud father, who can face the coming of a duster gas well or one good for 5,000,000 without shifting an eyelash..."

During the next half-century, Deemer produced and sold more natural gas to the United Natural Gas Company than any other independent producer in Pennsylvania. He prospected, opened several productive gas fields, and, for a time, held the world's record for cable tool depths.

162

In 1924 he planned to drill 3,200 feet down near Big Run. Not getting production, he continued drilling, to 4,000 feet, then to 5,280—a mile. He claimed it was then that the "Oriskany Bug" hit him. Oriskany sandstone is a geological feature common to West Virginia, Pennsylvania, and New York, and it is where oil and natural gas are found. When the well was abandoned in 1932, Deemer had worn out 60 drilling lines, three steam boilers, three steam engines, three bull wheel shafts, two band wheel shafts, and numerous crews and the well was 8,227 feet deep, the deepest cable tool hole in the world then.

Frank Clifton "Cliff" Deemer continued to set records in natural gas prospecting. When United Natural Gas Company officials acknowledged their more than 50 year business association in 1957, they presented him with a certificate that read, "For a period exceeding fifty years he has sold natural gas to the company in volumes exceeding those of any other independent producer in Pennsylvania. It is a unique but exemplary fact that through these many years of business association no written contract existed between the two. His word is his bond."

His word was his bond and many community institutions benefited from that word. He hosted the Olde Tyme Footballers Association annual reunion for many years. He made space available for both the Methodist Church congregation and for YMCA members when the buildings of those organizations burned. He also served on many community boards.

163

He and his wife, Anna Henderson, were the parents of Alexander D. Deemer II and Frank C. (Bob), Jr. Their interest in sports, work for their father in the natural gas and timber business, and the nation's emerging awareness of the environment led them to establish the Red Lick Preserve that maintains the pure watershed for Brookville. In the 1980s they founded Deemer Natural Resources for the conservation of natural resources.

The end result of that Oriskany Bug that began the search for a highly desired energy source more than a century ago is, for the people of Brookville, the source of our pure water supply today.

Frank Clifton "Cliff" Deemer lived his lifetime in Jefferson County. Photograph JCHS Collection

CLOTHES MAKE THE MAN!

RAY MCNEIL

1879—1970

A. Ray McNeil was a baseball player and a pro—but not the kind of pro most people think of when they think of baseball.

When baseball took off in the Brookville area about 1871, McNeil's family lived in Sigel. He grew up with the game and by the turn of the century, when he was a young man, 16 teams were playing as the American and National Leagues. By that time, too, a local league of young men was playing the circuit in this area, including a team from Sigel.

A newspaper photograph of that Sigel team includes A. Ray McNeil. Unfortunately, it is not dated. Local newspapers of that era did not have a weekly "sports page," so how can we find out when that Sigel team played ball?

An obituary and local directories tell us that McNeil was born in 1879 in Sigel, and attended both elementary and the academy there before going to Grove City College. He taught briefly before going to Philadelphia for his medical training. He began his practice in Sigel with Dr. Newcome in 1905, married in 1910, and became the physician for the Jefferson Coal Company in Beechwoods the same year.

When he and his wife returned to Brookville in 1916, they first lived at 128 Main Street (later Steele Electric and now used by

Matson's) where he also had his office. By 1927 they'd purchased a home at 24 South Main Street and he was practicing at 66 Pickering Street (now the Commonwealth Bank parking lot). Knowing these facts, we might assume a logical time for him to play ball would be when practicing medicine in Sigel before he married—the years between 1905 and 1910.

Besides his obituary and local directories there are other clues. Local players imitated the big leaguers and wore uniforms. Like the New York Knickerbockers, the first team to wear uniforms—white flannel shirts with black collars, blue woolen pantaloons, and straw hats in 1849—local teams were identified by what they wore.

One baseball writer estimates that more than 4,000 different uniform styles have been worn by major league ballplayers since 1876! Readers may be familiar with the red stockings worn first by the Cincinnati Red Stockings in 1868, or the checked uniforms first worn by the Brooklyn Bridegrooms in 1889, or the shield-fronted uniforms last worn by the Boston Beaneaters in 1897. Knowing uniform styles can help identify when a player may have played.

A. Ray McNeil's son and daughter-in-law used to spend their summers at the old McNeil home, where Marian would sort through family memorabilia. Then when it was time to return to Chevy Chase, Maryland, she would bring her treasures to the History Center—photographs and papers neatly identified and filed.

One summer she arrived carrying a big box. In it was the complete baseball uniform worn by her father-in-law, A. Ray McNeil. What a treasure it is to have that cap, jersey, pants, stockings, shoes, and everything else worn by this young man as he played with his team. And what wonderful clues this uniform offers!

Just what did A. Ray McNeil wear when he played for that Sigel team? Spalding's Baseball Guide for 1888 advertised muslin caps for 12 to 15 cents. Wool caps were more expensive—$2! McNeil wore the more expensive one with an abbreviated bill and forward-tilting crown typical of a "Boston-styled" baseball cap.

His gray wool flannel jersey had a collar and detachable long sleeves but was not the collarless jersey introduced in 1906. The pants ended at the knees and included belt loops—not the belt "tunnel" introduced in 1910 to avoid another player slowing a runner down! The belt was the customary brown leather, not the decorated stripes worn much earlier and the jersey was not numbered. That didn't happen until 1907 in the majors.

His sox had stripes and stirrups and were worn over "sanitaries," a style that first appeared in 1901. Sanitaries were white socks worn under the stirrup socks. Interestingly, sox cost more than caps—$4 a pair. The shoes are those typical of those worn for almost a century, brown leather with tri-cornered shoe plates on both heel and toe.

These wonderful clothing clues lead us to the conclusion that A. Ray McNeil did indeed play ball for Sigel, probably in 1905 and 1906. Newspapers show Sigel having a team both years, however players aren't listed.

People used to say, "Clothes make the man." In this case, clothes helped us identify when the man played ball! We now know that our pro, a "pro" by profession not a professional ball player, Dr. A. Ray McNeil, most likely played league baseball for Sigel in 1905 and 1906.

Players for the 1908 Ramsaytown team wore "Boston-style" caps, the customary dark belts, and sox over "sanitaries." They had not yet adopted the collarless jersey shirt that had been introduced two years previously.
Photographer unknown
Photograph JCHS Collection

A 19th CENTURY ARTIST'S WORK

1880

Following a March ice storm in 1939, a reporter turned to his typewriter and wrote, "Charley Bowdish never turned out a silver draped tree which could compare with the scintilant [sic] sparkling spectacle presented by every tree and shrub..."

Just blocks away at 170 Jefferson Street, Nell Clarke looked out her window and picked up her brush. Later that year, Nell entered her painting in a Milwaukee art show, where it earned favorable comments. Today, "Ice Storm," the watercolor she created, hangs in the Rebecca M. Arthurs Library.

Unlike many of the paintings in the History Center collection, she signed her work, so we know some things about her. She was born in 1878, graduated from Clarion Normal School, taught art in eastern schools, and died in 1970.

The History Center owns an oil portrait of Thomas K. Litch. A Massachusetts native, he moved from Pittsburgh to Brookville in 1850. He built his lumber mill at the confluence of the rivers, organized the Red Bank Navigation Company to keep the waterways open, and developed the bracket dam, a systematic way to create artificial flooding on shallow creeks.

Unfortunately like most of the 19th century art in the History Center collection, the artist who painted his portrait remains anonymous, and the date is unknown. The head and shoulders portrait is similar to Gilbert Stuarts' classical oil painting of George Washington, a dark, formally-posed older gentleman of means.

An engraving that is nearly identical appears in Kate Scott's 1888 history. Litch died in 1882 and, like the chicken and egg, we do not know which came first—the engraving or the painting. What we can surmise is that he did have his likeness produced either through a photograph, etching, or painting sometime during the 1870s or early 1880s.

When photography became popular during and after the Civil War, artists often copied from photographs. The History Center owns several charcoal portraits that were probably copied from 19th century photographs. Besides portraits, landscapes were common, and as photography became more popular, artists learned to tint them with colored pencils. The History Center owns a riverscape that we think is a photograph tinted by an anonymous artist. Probably created during the heyday of timbering in the 1880s, the riverscape includes two raft platforms in the water, one platform under construction, many house and buildings, and tiny people.

Some of these painters and photographers were itinerants, traveling and working from town to town. Many people here in the county own a "bird's-eye" print made by Thaddeus Mortimer Fowler (1842—1922), who learned photography during the Civil War. He and a man named Moyer traveled throughout parts of America photographing and sketching many towns. They were most prolific in Pennsylvania, where they created more than 250 "aerial" sketches, including Brookville in 1875. Fowler copyrighted his easily-recognizable prints.

In contrast, the earlier stencil artists who traveled through communities contributing their artistic talents to the walls in a community remain anonymous. One unknown stencil artist traveled through Brookville around 1868 when John McCracken was finishing the building now known as Landmark Square, at the southeast corner of Main and White Streets. In the ballroom on the third floor, the artist painted scenes and symbols depicting the story of the Civil War. Happily for us, they have been preserved.

Stonecutters left their art in many cemeteries that dot the county, and they, too remain anonymous, as do the woodworkers whose intricate designs embellish many of the 19th century homes throughout the county.

It is indeed unfortunate that so many of these 19th century artists remain unknown. Art created in the 20th century, like Nell Clarke's "Ice Storm," is usually signed and we are glad we can identify paintings by Burfoot, Craig, Youmans, Park, and others. We know, too, about photographers Clauser, Knapp and White.

The Jefferson County History Center is interested in documenting the art created in and about the county and urges county residents who have created or own artwork that can be attributed to Jefferson County to let us add the documentation to our computer database. Then in the distant future, when the time comes to hang art produced in the 20th or 21st century and related in some way to Jefferson County, the artists will no longer be anonymous.

Bridge at Cooksburg, one of the newer pieces in the History Center collection of art that relates to Jefferson County is Jason Lewis' painting. The artist lives in Clarion County but his topic is a well-known sight to those who live in Jefferson.

JCHC Collection

EXHIBITIONIST, BARNSTORMER, OR EXHIBITION FLYER?

LEWIS EARLE SANDT

1888—1913

First in Brookville to own a motorcycle. First to own an automobile. First in the United States to fly across Lake Erie and over the city of Pittsburgh. First to fly between Brookville and Punxsutawney. First American to make an international flight. Who was this man? Lewis Earle Sandt, born on May 18, 1888, and who died tragically at the age of twenty-five on June 22, 1913.

Brookville's Mary Geist Dick was a young girl when he took to the air. Later in life she reflected, "I must be truthful with you. Most people thought he was a little nutty. You see, that was the very early aviation. . . and the conservatives had not taken it up, shall we say, but the nutty one, like Earle, had." Was he, indeed, "a nutty one,"—an exhibitionist—someone who wanted to attract attention to himself?

Flying was in the air when Mary and Earle were growing up. In December 1903 Wilbur and Orville Wright flew their plane at Kitty Hawk. By 1907 Glenn Curtiss was involved with flight, and it didn't take long for him and the Wright brothers to realize the impact this new invention would have on the American public. By 1910 both had formed teams of exhibition flyers—

pilots who entertained crowds on the ground with daring feats in the air.

Sandt, the son of druggist George L. and Mary Verstine Sandt, grew up in the house at 42 South Pickering Street with three older siblings, Walter, Valetta, and Harriet. He was a so-so academic student preferring things mechanical. In 1909 the *Brookville Republican* observed, "There is mighty little that Earle doesn't know about the innards of an automobile."

He knew about the innards and evidently tested the machine's capabilities, for a year later the paper reported that "Earl [sic] Sandt, son of Mr. and Mrs. George L. Sandt, who is interested with his brother Walter in a garage in Erie met with an accident on Monday evening when he ran off a bridge in North East in a car, sustaining some severe bruises and lacerations. Latest advices are that he is not seriously wounded, and will be able to be about in a few days."

Not content with bicycles and automobiles, he turned to airplanes in 1911 and soon was in the air. He entered the Curtiss School of Flying in Hammondsport, N.Y. where Curtiss himself taught him to fly during a six-week course. Sandt returned to Erie with a new $4,500 Curtiss bi-plane and on Thanksgiving Day flew it to the delight of friends and neighbors.

Several months later Sandt gathered Erie newsmen together and told them he intended to be a greater pilot than Lincoln Beachey, then Curtiss' leading aviator. During the next eighteen months he was well on his way. He was the first to fly from Erie to Canada, completing the round trip with a crash near North East. He wasn't hurt but the plane was lost. During 1912 he flew exhibitions. He flew over Pittsburgh, taking off from Schenley Park, and took off from Walnut Street in Brookville on a flight to Punxsutawney. He flew the first airmail for the state of Ohio. In June of 1913 he flew an exhibition in Grove City, crashed, and then developed lockjaw as the result of a broken leg. Serum arrived too late and Lewis Earle Sandt died at 25.

Just as Sandt had tested the capabilities of the automobiles he drove, he tested the capabilities of the planes he flew. He flew them higher. He flew them farther. He flew them in difficult weather. He manipulated them in new ways. Aviation historian David H. Onkst wrote "Although early exhibition aviators entertained millions and helped spur popular interest in flight, some scholars estimate that the fatality rate among them was as high as 90 percent. For those early aviators who never became rich, famous, or even well known, that was an expensive price to pay."

So was this Brookville man a barnstormer, an exhibition flyer, or as Mary Geist Dick referred to him—"a nutty one"—an exhibitionist? The date of his death rules out "barnstormer," a term that describes a pilot who would land in a farmer's field, gather a crowd, and do stunts, and that didn't originate until after Sandt died.

Local folks might have described him as an exhibitionist, a person who wants to attract attention to him or herself, but the newspapers and magazines of his time didn't. The Pittsburgh Post said, "Risking his life to the treachery of a gale and battling the elements, Earle Sandt thrilled the city by his spectacular flight," and the *Scientific American* said, "That he escaped with his life after his perilous trip is well nigh miraculous." Yet he bragged to reporters that he would be a greater pilot than Beachey.

Exhibition flyers, on the other hand, were interested in demonstrating to others the capabilities of this new invention. Today, flight historians like Onkst describe these exhibition flyers as "courageous individuals who experimented with the limits of aeroplane design at a time when many designers were still struggling to solve some of the most fundamental aeronautical engineering problems."

We conclude that Brookville born Lewis Earle Sandt (pictured with a bandaged hand) was one of these "courageous individuals," with just a tad of exhibitionism thrown into the mix!

DANCING THE NIGHT AWAY
1890—1990

The enjoyment of dancing in Brookvillegoes back a long time to the days of barn dances and frolics. Barns are certainly large enough, but what other spaces have been used by those folks who enjoyed dancing? Keep in mind that for some pioneers, dancing, like playing cards, was not an acceptable form of entertainment!

Commercial buildings on Main Street like McCracken Hall and the YMCA had large rooms for balls and hops, but so do many residences. Ever wonder why so many older homes in Brookville are three stories high? Take a walk along Jefferson Street, Euclid Avenue, or South Pickering and you will see houses with mansard or pitched roofs, and third-floor gable windows that reflect the sun on bright winter days. Some third floors had rooms for live-in servants, but many of those windows are in the ballrooms.

Frank and Mary Fleeger owned the Litch Mansion between 1968 and 1995. When interviewed in 1980, they pointed out that at one time, "the third floor played host to many gala affairs and was decorated and furnished for just such occasions." Unfortunately the structure had been vacant for many years when they bought it, and the third floor had been stripped of the cut glass chandelier, parquet flooring, and concert grand piano that once graced the interior, but one can imagine the elegant folks of yesteryear waltzing or dancing a quadrille there after a sumptuous meal on the first floor.

The present History Center does not have a third floor nor was it built as a house. Instead it housed retail stores on the first floor and the apartment of the Edelblute family on the second. The room that now houses the Bowdish Model Railroad Exhibit was the ballroom and the band or orchestra played from the adjacent "skylight" room. In 1890 when Ada Edelblute married Elmer Pearsall more than 200 people came to the wedding, enjoyed dinner, and then danced the night away. Might they have danced to a new and lively ragtime or a cakewalk?

During the 1921 Brookville Fair, the American Legion hosted a day for "the doughboys and gobs from this section." Strenuous pursuits filled the day, and in the evening, there was dancing, perhaps dancing the foxtrot, in the "third story of the Leathers garage." The building on Madison Street (since demolished) had just been completed and boasted "25,000 feet of floor space or "one of the largest dancing floors in this section of the state. A Cleveland orchestra provided the music, perhaps playing popular songs like "You're The Cream in My Coffee" or "Ain't We Got Fun?"

The Charleston and tango epitomize the Roaring Twenties, and so does dancing with many partners. Dance cards in our collections are signed by the young men who wished to dance with some of the local sweethearts. During the Great Depression, young people danced in school gyms and the YMCA, or traveled to a

178

dance hall in Reynoldsville. Big band music was popular and teacher C. H. Cooper taught young men to play instruments— enough, in fact, to form a group called the Sunshine Boys. They played in the school gym, the Masonic Hall, and the Brookville Park Auditorium Building or "White Elephant" during the annual fair.

World War II saw the continuation of swing and the advent of the jitterbug as people continued to dance the night away. When the Western Pennsylvania Laurel Festival resumed in 1959, the Queen's Ball was a formal event with live music at Pinecrest Country Club, an event that continued into the mid-eighties. Square dancing in the high school gym and teen dances in the Northside School gym brought the crowds out to dance to fiddle tunes and local DJs.

When Brookville's Victorian Christmas Celebration began more than two decades ago, it didn't take long for folks to organize a Victorian Ball. My very favorite took place on the third floor of McCracken Hall, now called Landmark Square. It was a snowy night and the ballroom was heated by an assortment of electric heaters. Frost quickly formed around the electric candles in the window, but the room temperature did not slow the grand march of ladies in hoops and taffeta and men in uniform. It was a grand event that recalled in a lovely way, the pleasure of folks dancing through the night so many years ago!

Filling out a dance card for both young women and young men was an important part of formal dances in the early part of the 20th century.
Photographer Frederick E. Knapp, Brookville
Courtesy Brookville Heritage Trust

BE MY VALENTINE
1893

Many teachers say that kids get more excited over Valentine's Day than any other holiday. That shouldn't be hard to understand when considering the importance we humans place on being loved and of loving someone else. The paper valentine is just one of the many ways people express that love.

One explanation for this special day that features love and romance has young Romans in the third century sending messages to their sweethearts following the execution of a priest named Valentine on February 14, 270 A.D. Earlier when the Roman army faced a shortage of virile young men to serve, Claudius II had banned marriage for them. Valentine protested, performed marriages, and was imprisoned. Awaiting execution he penned a note to the daughter of his jailer and signed it, "From Your Valentine."

Chaucer later linked Valentine's Day with romance upon the marriage of Richard II to Anne of Bohemia. Shakespeare refers to it, too. By the 18th century English lovers were sending each other gifts and handmade cards. Hand-painted valentines appeared in the first part of the 19th century in the United States. When Esther Howland imported fancy papers and laces from Europe in the 1830s and mass-produced cards in Massachusetts, the custom of exchanging valentines took off in earnest.

With the exception of penny dreadfuls, 19th century cards were elaborate. The most elaborate card in the History Center's Valentine collection measures 7 ½ by 12 ½ inches and can be displayed upright, like a framed photograph. Trimmed with flowers, scrolled paper, a cut-out butterfly, the message is simply "Hearts Desire." It is not signed but is very typical of cards printed in Germany after the Civil War using a technique called chromolithography. Penny dreadfuls or vinegar valentines became popular right before the Civil War. These were derogatory cards without fancy trimmings that sold for one penny.

Hallmark is the name many associate with cards today, but it was Norcross that came up with printed paper valentines around the turn of the century. The Norcross card in the History Center's collection is small, a folded 3x4" card printed in red, "To you, From me, With Love," and signed Betty H. That same Betty H. also signed a hand painted card decorated with heart-shaped flowers. The envelope is handmade from red construction paper and is carefully addressed to Elizabeth Anne Sandt.

Two unusual cards are both pink. The first is in book form with "How to Make Love in Many Countries" on the cover. The pages done in black and red on white contain poetry describing the courtship of Eskimos, Spaniards, Italians, Arabians, and Chinese and is signed "Tommy." The second is postcard size but has its own beautifully lined envelope. The verse commands, "Take me--discriminate!" and is signed Clarence Heckman.

In the 1930s her students must have loved Miss Dorothy Horner and she must have loved them for we have a number of cards signed in their very best cursive. Some are trimmed with paper lace. Others, like those fancy Christmas bells, become three-dimensional when opened.

One local paper mentioned "Valentine day" in 1893 and Sandt's drugstore advertised the "Bonaza line of Valentines!" in 1899. By 1908 Sandt's promoted the "latest comics, post cards and artistic creations in silks, etc." At the same time jeweler and optician Guth knew that Valentine's Day was an appropriate occasion for proposals of marriage and advertised "Diamonds for engagement rings $25 and up."

By 1922 the paper valentine apparently wasn't enough and merchants saw an opportunity to promote candy and flowers, too. Heart-shaped candy boxes became popular during World War II and a regular recipe column in the Brookville American told how to make a heart-shaped meat and vegetable pie for that special someone.

Local merchants continued to capitalize on the day. Dan Smith promoted "Candy to Pamper Her" and to tell her "how sweet she is" in 1958, while Brookville Creamery promoted "Cupid's favorite flavors." Not wishing to be left out, Brown's Boot Shop suggested nylon stockings at $.79, $.89 or $1.00, and Rubin's thought "Valentine frills from our lingerie collection" might fit the bill. And all three drug stores reminded youngsters that "valentines were never such fun!" whether they made their own or bought ready-mades. The valentine—still a lovely custom when signed simply "From Your Valentine."

Someone sent sixty-year old Jennie Pinney this "penny dreadful" Valentine in 1910. Her daughter, Rhea or Rebecca, married Sam Arthurs and they lived on Main Street. After her death, Rebecca Arthurs endowed her home as a public library for Brookville.

JCHS Collection

FROM MAN TO MYTH
CHARLES ALBERT BOWDISH
1896–1988

Most older folks in this area know the story. When young Charlie Bowdish returned from Europe where he'd been gassed, he was too ill to work so he built a little miniature village with a train for his brother's wedding. More than 600 people came to see it in 1920 and that was the beginning of his annual Christmas shows at his home south of the White Street Bridge.

That's the myth—the stories that have grown up about the man who originated what has become the Miniature Railroad & Village™ at the Carnegie Science Center in Pittsburgh. Myth serves an important function in every culture. Here in rural Pennsylvania, the story of an injured veteran who loved children and entertained them and their families year after year without charging a dime is an inspired story of self-giving and one that resonates as each Christmas season rolls around.

But what are the facts? And how did the Bowdish story become the myth it is for some folks today?

Bowdish grew up in Brookville with two older brothers, two older sisters, and his parents. His forebears had moved into the Brockway area where they were skillful machinists, woodworkers, and musicians. This we know

185

from the family genealogy and an article written in 1899 by Pittsburgh reporter Bion Butler.

Like many in the 19th century, Charlie's parents yearned for new horizons. In their early married life they traveled to Michigan and Nebraska. The birthplaces of their children help us know this. Charlie was born in Brookville in 1894, 1895, 1896, 1897, or 1898! Here the facts are confusing because census records and other information cite various years—1900 census says 1894, 1910 census says 1895, 1920 census 1897, and 1930 says 1898. The family genealogy lists February 28, 1895 and his tombstone at the Baptist Cemetery in Richardsville says February 28, 1896, but even tombstones are sometimes wrong! His signed social security application says 1896 and that is the date the History Center uses.

School records for Charlie are hard to find and newspapers do not list him among the graduates. Newspapers do list him as #342 of draftees in 1917 and we know he left for Camp Lee, Virginia, shortly before his 22nd birthday. Like other young men his age, Charlie must have been proud to enter the military. Wearing his uniform, he posed for pictures at Knapp's Studio on Main Street. Later he sent the editor of the *Brookville American* a photograph of Camp Lee and then appeared himself several days later, saying he'd strained a "heart muscle" and was on a sixty-day furlough.

A copy of Charlie's honorable discharge paper dated July 12, 1920, however, shows that his military service was terminated due to "valvular heart disease, incurred not in line of duty." In other words Charlie had a heart problem that may have been present from birth or caused by an infection. He did not return to Camp Lee, and he did not travel to Europe where the war raged, and he did not suffer the ill effects of mustard gas.

Instead his parents encouraged him to take over the responsibility of creating the annual Christmas exhibit that his father, Albert, had done for years. Even before electricity was common, Albert had created special displays with moving figures powered by a windmill!

Charlie did and when his brother, George, married Mae Loesser on Christmas Day of 1919 friends did see his work and word did spread thanks to Alfred Truman. The Carnegie Science Center says Charlie's first exhibit was in 1920. Was it? George and Mae's marriage is described in the *Jeffersonian Democrat* in January of 1920, an easy mistake for someone doing quick research to make, but the wedding described in the January 1920 newspaper had occurred the month before, on December 25, 1919.

Did 600 people come as reported in Pennsylvania Profiles in 1989? Charlie himself recalled in an interview by David Putnam that about 400 came and he enjoyed it! "It wasn't anything out of the ordinary but around 400 visited our home that Christmas season to view the display and that attention got me started."

The facts about the man or the myth? Does it matter when bright-eyed children catch

187

the fun when the rooster crows and the trains begin to run on the Bowdish Model Railroad Layout at the History Center? Probably not! For historians, though, and for adults the facts should be important.

Bowdish was an actor in his father's stock company prior to enlisting in 1917.

Courtesy Greg Becker, Brookville

When on leave the next spring he posed for Brookville photographer Frederick E. Knapp. Honorably discharged due to a heart murmur, he began his life's work of miniatures and models.

Families and friends looked forward to an annual visit to see what Bowdish had created for the holidays.

Bowdish moved his railroad exhibit to Buhl Planetarium in 1954. In 1980 (right) he was still building miniatures and overseeing the building of the annual Christmas exhibit there. Today the exhibit has expanded and become the Miniature Railroad & Village™ at the Carnegie Science Center.
Photographs JCHS Collection

Charles Albert Bowdish 1896-1988

BOWDISH WRITES
1896—1988

Machinist, electrician, woodworker, photographer, miniaturist, creative genius! Each has described Charles Albert Bowdish, the man behind the Miniature Railroad & Village™ at the Carnegie Science Center. Very few descriptions, however, describe him as a writer.

Bowdish was born before the turn of the 20th century, witnessed the wars of the twentieth century as a citizen, and lived through both good and bad economic times. As he grew older he sat at his typewriter and reflected on his lifetime and what was happening around him. Those reflections took the form of letters to the editor that were printed in the local papers.

From his letters, we can get a sense of the man and his beliefs.

Bowdish had created an annual Christmas exhibit in his home at 8 White Street in Brookville for more than three decades before moving it to Pittsburgh in 1954. The sixties gave birth to war in Vietnam, uprisings among American youth and women, and a statewide teacher strike.

Charles, who admitted he enjoyed the attention he got from his exhibits, felt isolated. He penned a letter to the editor complaining that he'd been "turned out to pasture without one word of thanks for a job well done," and signed it the "old-fashioned feller who still eats supper."

He usually signed his letters with one form or other of "Charles Bowdish, the old fashioned fellow that still eats supper," a reflection of his rural roots where "dinner" was the noon meal and "supper" was eaten in the evening.

He continued writing, sometimes one, more often two or three letters each year to the local papers. These letters reveal him as a fiscal conservative, political independent, and patriot. He was uninterested in accumulating wealth yet would be beholding to no one, and surprisingly, he was a supporter of women's rights. But most of all, he was a passionate and fundamental believer and a lover of an old-fashioned Christmas.

Bowdish always thought government spending an abomination and criticized both Republicans and Democrats alike. In 1982 he wrote, "With the greed and arrogance of some of our public officials is it any wonder we get the idea that when some of them were born the good doctor made a mistake and slapped the wrong end too hard."

His father had promoted "a good show cheap" not a cheap show, so he found the loosening morals of television, movies, and Broadway shows like *Hair* anathema. When the country celebrated the Bicentennial in 1976, he declared his patriotism and wrote "A prayer for my country—Almighty God, keep your protecting hand over American, so we may pass on to those who come after us the heritage of a free people, and the day never come when we will be ashamed or afraid to say, I AM AN AMERICAN."

Bowdish remembered growing up with two sisters and a mother, all of whom were fully involved in the Bowdish Stock Company at the same time women were fighting for the vote. He favored equal opportunities for women, and wrote, "We need women in every office (and I don't mean just clerks). Isn't it time for big daddy to recognize women for what they are, intellectual equals?...Isn't it time for man to recognize the equality of the other half of society?"

He never charged for his Brookville exhibits, although some local folks recall making donations, and wasn't concerned about accumulating wealth. "I have been told many times that I could be a wealthy man if I knew how to charge....I am rich beyond compare. I have a home to keep—more than work worth doing—wonderful friends—contentment—peace of mind—good health. Anyone with wealth like that—owns much—it can never be bought or sold."

Some local folks reacted sharply and he occasionally received unsigned letters of criticism. His tart response was simply, "The Bowdish family has always worked hard and paid for everything they ever had and has always given freely of their talents (and they have many) when ever asked."

Bitter towards society in his later years, during his lifetime Charles Albert Bowdish had combined his love of entertainment and his mechanical and artistic genius to create exhibits viewed by millions who shared his love of Christmas and his passionate faith, and by many who simply admired his exceptional artistic skill.

Each fall he would sit at his typewriter on the second floor of the house at 8 White Street and type a Christmas message for his exhibit programs. Once he wrote, "May there come to you and yours not only this Christmas day, but every day, an abundance of the most precious things of life, good health and enduring friendships," and that is our wish, too, to our readers.

SPACES FOR SPORT
1904

Traveling west on I-80, drivers and passengers who look to the north see the green oval of an athletic field surrounded by the deep red track. The opposing sets of bleachers rise on either side. East of the competitive athletic field are practice areas for a variety of sports, all carefully cared for by the maintenance staff.

A century ago, of course, when sports like football were just making their way into the lives of high school boys, there was no I-80 and the present school campus was the farmland of Vaughn Hawk.

Instead, Brookville students attended the old Central School that perched upon "knowledge knob," where the Northside Park is today. The original building was built in 1878 to educate students in grades 1 through 8. The high school organized in 1883 and the first graduation class earned diplomas in 1886.

It took time for athletics to develop at the high school, but enthusiasm for the game that had begun at Yale in 1876 was growing and in 1893 Brookville High School organized a football team. Where did these players play?

In 1898 the Central School building expanded with the addition of the Paul Darling Memorial Hall. It included 4 classrooms and an auditorium but no gymnasium. The first annex added in 1923 included 6 more classrooms and

2 labs. A second annex in 1928 added 5 more classrooms, a library, a gymnasium, and a domestic science area. Photographs exist of these buildings, but it is difficult to know the layout of the exterior property. Was there ever a football field on "knowledge knob?"

Local newspapers didn't devote a full section to sports then, but a 1904 column listing local happenings briefly reports that the Brookville High School team had defeated a team from Clarion Normal (then a two-year teacher training school) on Allgeier's Meadow. The Allgeiers had a brewery on Race Street, and a phone call to a descendent reassured us that we can assume those early football games were played on the flat land on the south side of the Red Bank.

In the early days football was an increasingly aggressive sport. There was grave concern from President Theodore Roosevelt on down to local coaches when, in one year, nineteen young men died from injuries suffered while playing in games across the nation. The local editor commented more than once about the dangers of the game and eventually football ceased in Brookville and basketball and track became *the* sports. But where did both boys and girls play basketball as early as 1906? The Paul Darling Memorial Hall contained an auditorium. Was it also used as a gymnasium?

By 1925 football rules had changed, and in Brookville school leaders organized a high school athletic association to encourage, organize, and guide all branches of physical and athletic competitions in the school. It took a while, but in 1929, the school board hired Joseph Barnett to direct football, basketball, and track.

Photographs of Coach Barnett and his team could have been taken anywhere, so once again we are left with the question—where did the Raiders play?

For basketball, the answer is more readily answered. Charles Elliott "Andy" Hastings excelled in football, baseball, basketball, and track at the University of Pittsburgh where he ranks as one of their all-time stars. In 1939 the gymnasium that was built in 1928 was dedicated as the Andy Hastings Gymnasium.

The Brookville High School football team of 1948 poses on Allgeier's meadow (aka the "flats") with coaches Nedwidek (right) and Chilcott (left front), manager Bill Smith (left middle), and high school principal Hassan Rockey (left rear).
JCHS Collection

Thousands of girls and boys have learned to swim in the indoor pool at the Brookville YMCA. Since 1971, indoor swimming has also been available at the Hickory Grove Elementary School pool.
Courtesy YMCA

LAST ONE IN IS A ROTTEN EGG!
1905—2016

What's more fun and more refreshing than jumping into cold water on a hot summer day? Kids have enjoyed the old swimming hole for time immemorial, and in Brookville for more than a century, that old swimming hole has been "the dam" at Dr. Walter Dick Memorial Park.

In 1900 the sprawling Litch lumber mill occupied the North Fork area above the East Main Street bridge, and old photographs show the millpond above the bracket dam. The millpond, of course, was too dangerous for swimming, but 19th century sources refer to the area north of the millpond as "dark hollow," and it was there that many boys went to swim unguarded.

They swam in the numerous streams of the area, too, as evidenced by numerous reports of drowning. For example, in 1905 an 18-year-old drowned in Little Toby Creek when he was "seized with cramps" and sank into a deep hole. In 1911 a man drowned "in a small stream from cramps," and in 1915 a 21-year-old drowned in a Porter Township stream. Others drowned in the larger rivers like the Clarion.

On the west side of the lumber mill's pond, a group of men, who had privately incorporated in 1883 to provide Brookville homes with water, had built a pumping station and installed an intake pipe. The Litch mill closed in

1905 and by 1912 the borough had purchased the water company and completed a new filtration plant and concrete and earthenwork dam, both familiar to us today.

Girls began to join the boys there to swim, and so did grown-ups. Concerns about cleanliness arose. In 1915 a local editor wrote, "the boys and girls as well as the older folks who enjoy swimming have been requesting council on various occasions to erect bath houses adjoining the swimming pool south of the water works dam on the North Fork." The borough fathers responded by inspecting the location, ordering lumber for two bathhouses, and assuming all expenses.

Water safety was another concern. Even before the present indoor pool was built there, the Y offered swim classes. "The swimming classes usually conducted by the YMCA will start next Monday morning at 10:00 o'clock. Secretary Bartholemew will be in charge and no boys will be permitted in the water unless he is present. The swimming will be done in the North Fork as last year." More than 100 boys had been in the previous year's class, and 40 had learned to swim. Once the Y pool was completed swimming classes for both boys and girls were an annual occurrence.

Summer swimming at the dam continued to be popular but there was also enthusiasm to have a pool. A committee of local businessmen and community members solicited funds at $10 a share in the summer of 1928 to build a swimming pool "plenty big enough for a community of this size." It would be located at the Park entrance (the present Memorial Park) near Red Bank Creek and have "a beach of white sand along one side." Inlet and outlet pipes would be of the same size so the water would be constantly changing. There would be a wading pool, too. Needless to mention, that pool never materialized.

The floods of 1936 and the 1996 did severe damage to the dam area, and in the first case, Dr. Walter Dick himself, and in the second, his family, contributed financially and motivationally to restore and improve the area for swimming. In an oral interview Mary Geist Dick remembered, "They didn't have many places to go [for swimming] and so my husband was very partial to the park. He thought swimming was a great sport that all children should learn." After his death, the Dick family donated substantial funds for the park's development and the area was named after him.

There was no swimming at the dam for several years after the 1936 flood. The Y, however, had offered free swimming lessons beginning in 1933 funded by Fulton Chevrolet. Nearly 500 youngsters took advantage of these free programs, even though the Y didn't "guarantee to make a Lenore Kight or Johnny Weismuller out of every pupil," but it did guarantee "an opportunity for practice under the best possible conditions of safety and sanitation." Kight and Weismuller were famous Olympic swimmers in the thirties.

To cool off today in a safe and healthy way, a multitude of choices exist both indoors and out. The dam at Dr. Walter Dick Memorial Park is still maintained by the borough. There is a pool at Cook Forest and cold spring water at Clear Creek. The YMCA offers lessons for people of all ages, and if you're lucky, you may even have a pool in your own back yard! So come on in, the water's fine!

The dam swimming area at Dr. Walter Dick Memorial Park is maintained by the borough of Brookville, and, over the years, has been assisted by civic organizations like the Kiwanis Club, the Lions, and the North Fork Watershed Association. In 1972 kids of all ages flocked there to swim, hunt for crayfish, sunbathe, and just have fun.

McMurray Collection
JCHS

THAT LONG FOOTBALL HIATUS
1906—1936

The Steelers report to St. Vincent's the end of July to prepare for their opening game. The Nittany Lions and Pitt Panthers ready for their opening games, and in Brookville the Raiders practice prior to their opening game. It is August.

A century ago though, in 1908, there were no Raiders. There was no high school football team for that was the year the football hiatus began.

Walter Camp, Yale's football coach in 1876, is credited with the origin of the game that "typifies the American competitive spirit in its premium upon imagination, speed, strategy and daring, as well as upon sheer physical ability and durability."

The sport itself is a modification of the European games of soccer and rugby. It was Camp who wrote the rules and shaped the game for America. Soon local athletic clubs in Pittsburgh were having intense competitions, and by the end of the century players competed professionally, in colleges, and even in mining communities like Eleanora and Coal Glen. With so much football in the air, younger boys wanted to play, too.

Brookville's Central School was built in 1878 and the first graduation occurred 8 years later.

The first football team was organized in 1893. Some teachers in those days were called "Professor." In 1901 Prof. Downs and Prof. Kramlich coached and managed a team captained by Herb Neel.

The local newspapers didn't devote a full section to sports then, but in a 1904 column devoted to local happenings, the editor reported that the Brookville High School team had defeated a team from Clarion Normal (then a two-year teacher training school) on Allgeiers Meadow. He added it was "a good clean game and a great credit to our high school team." The following week he reported one player had sprained a wrist when beaten by Punxsutawney, but "the game was clean throughout and closely contested."

In those days football was an even more rough and tumble game than it is today because the protective uniforms of today did not exist. At a 1958 event attorney Raymond Brown recalled coming to Brookville in 1905 as a struggling young lawyer, where he was asked to organize and coach a football team. The team used cast-off clothing as uniforms to play a schedule that included teams from both Clarion and Indiana Normal.

Fans followed college games and knew about plays like the flying wedge, a strategy that involved massive charges by one team against the other that sometimes resulting in serious injury. By 1905 when Brown was asked to coach there was nationwide concern after 19 fatalities occurred. President Theodore Roosevelt threatened to shut the game down and, locally, as the 1906 was about to begin, editor John McMurray wrote, "We are sorry to announce that the football season begins in a few days. Just keep an account of the accidents and fatalities. They will surprise you."

Indiana Normal beat DuBois High School 6-5 that season. The next season when a DuBois player ended a game with a cracked jawbone and a visitor had his nose broken, McMurray wrote, "This game is barbarous and ought to be abolished."

And in Brookville, it was. The football hiatus began and sports fans turned to basketball and track.

By 1925 football rules had changed. In Brookville's school leaders organized a high school athletic association to encourage, organize, and guide all branches of physical and athletic competitions in the school. It took a while, but in 1929, the school board hired Joseph Barnett to direct football, basketball, and track. The new athletic coach came from North East and set to work to develop a team.

It was, of course, an uphill battle. There was no tradition. When the Maroon and White eleven met the Clarion High School team on the Brookville Park grounds on a fall afternoon, it was "the first football season that the school had seen in many years." Brookville lost to Clarion in the opener of a six-game series. Their lack of experience led to more defeats until they managed to beat Ashland Township High School and Falls Creek both 20-0.

In the Ashland game Brookville's Sellers had fractured his right leg in a mix-up with visitors, so editor John McMurray was happy to report the following week that "at no time did visitors seriously threaten the Brookville goal line." Then the final game with Franklin was cancelled due to the scarlet fever epidemic that closed down school and community. The season ended 2 wins, 4 losses.

Coach Barnett continued to build his team: 3 wins, 5 losses in both 1930 and 1931; 2 wins, 6 losses in 1932. Then came the wonderful undefeated season of 1933, the first undefeated season in Brookville's history! Barnett ended his Brookville career with seasons of 8 wins, 1 loss, and 5 wins, 3 losses, before moving on in 1936.

It took several seasons before Brookville had another undefeated team. Here's wishing this year's team well! Go Raiders!

Note: While researching this article we found reference to "motion pictures taken by F. C. McFadden of Coach Barnett's football teams in action." The History Center is interested in tracking their whereabouts.

Brookville's football team of 1905 wore cast-off clothing instead of uniforms when they posed for a postcard photograph.

Postcard
JCHS Collection

Joe Barnett came to Brookville in 1929 to restart the football program. Photograph donation of Joe Barnett, jr.

HOW WILL YOU SPEND NEW YEAR'S EVE?

1906-1971

Following the midnight ringing of bells and firing of guns in 1906, someone in town complained, "The good citizens of Brookville don't object to the ringing of bells, firing of guns, etc. on New Year's, and the Fourth of July...But they do object to having the fire bell rung at midnight on these occasions, startling them by the awful alarm of fire. This was done Sunday night of this week."

Bells have been used for both warning and celebration over the centuries. In Brookville, the courthouse bell called citizens to fight fire and also signaled the end of war. And once upon a time, it pealed as the old year ended, and the New Year began. We presume the town fathers remedied the problem of 1906 so as not to alarm the community, but how else did folks celebrate?

Many local churches held watch-nights— times for people to contemplate the year past and the year ahead. In 1906 for example, the Methodist Episcopalians held a watch-night and "many stayed until midnight." In 1928, both Baptists and the Methodist Episcopalians held them. More than a half century later, in 1961, the First Assembly of God held a watch-night and showed the film "Martin Luther" prior to a New Year's Eve Communion Service. For some church groups, the evening was more social.

One year the ladies of the Jefferson United Presbyterian Church honored the pastor's wife and presented her with a new bedspread, embroidered with more than 100 names of members and friends. [If anyone knows the whereabouts of this bedspread, the History Center would welcome a call.]

Both the Columbia Theater and the YMCA were popular places where Brookville folks congregated during much of the 20th century, and both capitalized on New Year's Eve and New Year's Day. In 1927 the Columbia advertised "movies at the stroke of 12," followed by a song and dance review on stage, "Brookville on Parade." The film, "265 Nights in Hollywood" starred James Dunn and Alice Faye. In 1960, the grand sum of 30 cents would purchase admission to 25 cartoons, "Psycho," and "Time Machine."

In 1906, before the present Y building was constructed, a "reception at the YMCA room on Monday [New Year's Day] was largely attended." A "fine program" was in the works for New Year's Day in 1934.

Other people welcomed the New Year by dancing, bowling, or skating. The Edgewood Park Roller Rink in DuBois advertised in the Brookville papers and provided "hats and noisemakers," while the Gateway Bowling Center in Brookville offered "noisemakers, hats, and all the trimmings for lots of fun."

Many groups used the changing of the years as an opportunity to entertain. In 1928 the

YMCA was the setting for a supper for the Brotherhood of Local Firemen and Engineers and the Ladies' Society. The supper was followed with round and square dancing and cards at Matson's Hall. The next afternoon the Reverend and Mrs. Shoemaker entertained at a reception at the Presbyterian manse. In 1960 the Intermediate Class of the Church of Christ held a New Year's Day party at Stockdale Cabins.

Some folks celebrated by dining with family and friends. Riverside Market reminded folks that pork was just 35 cents a pound and sauerkraut 3 pounds for 39 cents for "that traditional pork and sauerkraut meal." And for the non-cooks, the Gold Eagle reminded folks in 1971 they'd observe the New Year by serving the "traditional pork and sauerkraut."

Wishing people a "Happy New Year" as well as looking back and reflecting on the past, and looking forward to starting anew on January 1 have been part of New Year's customs, too. Like today, local newspapers used their advertising space to send their good wishes to readers, and, like folks today, people a century ago made New Year's resolutions. And, like us, broke them quickly, according to one editor who wrote in January, "How about those New Year's resolutions you adopted? The ink on them was hardly dry when you began to go back on them."

Whether you make resolutions, set off firecrackers, attend a watch-night service, have dinner with friends, or cozy up to the television to watch the New Year come in on Times Square, we hope your New Year's celebration is a pleas-

211

ant one. We do know one thing for sure—the bell in the courthouse cupola will not ring! The folks in 1906 saw to that!

The Jefferson County Courthouse as it appeared around 1910, several years after citizens complained about the ringing of the cupola bell on New Year's Eve.
Postcard JCHS Collection

REMEMBER WHEN GIRLS WORE BLOOMERS?

1906—1972

As curator half my time is spent with the collections—the objects, photographs, and documents that the Historical Society owns and cares for. We appraise them by asking how might they help us show the stories of Jefferson County. We describe them by listing their quantity, quality, size, materials, and more. We clean and repair them and store them in acid-free folders and boxes. And we exhibit them.

It is tedious, but also lots of fun. A volunteer prior to 2004 accomplished much of the documentation and scanning of photographs taken by Brookville photographer Frederick Knapp between 1898 and 1945, but a box or two remained unscanned. One included pictures of Brookville High School basketball teams, both boys and girls, and while I scanned them these images got me thinking about the evolution of this all-American sport and its beginnings, particularly for girls, in our local high school.

Basketball originated in Massachusetts in 1891 when Canadian James Naismith compiled the rules for the boys at the YMCA Training School in Springfield, Massachusetts. By the next year, the girls at Smith College were playing the game, too. So how long did it take this new sport to reach rural Jefferson County?

213

Some pictures in the Knapp Collection were dated, the earliest being 1906 for both boys and girls basketball teams. The girls' dark bloomers reached their knees and their tops had sleeves. The boys' uniforms bared both arms and legs. A 1906 *Jeffersonian Democrat* item anticipated a January trip for both teams to play the teams at "Beechwoods" or Washington Township Vocational School, all part of the "recently organized Jefferson County high school league for championship honors." Two years earlier the boys had traveled to Beechwoods too, but then there was nary a mention of the girls. Brookville students produced a periodical called *The Periscope*. In one issue, they wrote about the boys' basketball games. In fact, the 1920 spring issue lists all ten games, then adds "thus far the girls team has played but three games, two with Clarion and one with Corsica," and continues, "But for the work of Darr as forward the game would have smelled very badly." Now, my mother-in-law did tell me once she'd played basketball in bloomers as a BHS student, but she didn't tell me she was the second-stringer who made the team look pretty good on at least one occasion!

Boys' varsity basketball continued to be very popular, particularly because there had not been a football team since 1906. In fact, between 1906 and 1929 basketball was *the* sport all over town! In 1927 Brookville played teams from DuBois, Punxsutawney, Kittanning, Indiana, and Erie East. Local papers carried the scores on the front page of both the high school games and of the highly competitive YMCA team games. In

December, for example, the Brookville Y Team beat the Chicago YMCA College Team, 35 to 27.

Girls continued to play, too, but not as extensively as the boys. The 1927 *Echo* explained that "during the mid-part of each school term, a short period of time is devoted to a girls' interclass basketball tournament," and included photographs of the girls wearing light-colored middies, ties, and bloomers. The Junior girls won the title that year. When the new gym opened in 1929, it was "hoped that in the future we will have a girls' varsity." However, the earlier Jefferson County High School league seemed to have faded from view for only the Girl's Interclass Basketball games are mentioned.

By the end of World War II, boys were playing varsity, junior varsity, and junior high basketball, and the Little Imps or varsity girls were playing against Summerville, Clearfield, and Clarion teams. Then girls' basketball disappeared, not to resume until the mid-sixties.

Under Title IX in 1972, educational opportunities for girls in high schools and colleges increased substantially, as did sports coverage in our local newspapers. Now, we have pages devoted to games played by both boys and girls of all ages.

As for the bloomers the girls once wore— well, thankfully, they've been replaced by uniforms that are similar to the uniforms worn by boys. However, if you happen to have a pair of bloomers in your attic, we'd like to have them!

While not identical, all their uniforms did have long-sleeves, wide collars, and bloomers when these Brookville girls posed during the 1906 basketball season.
Photographer Frederick E. Knapp, Brookville
Courtesy Brookville Heritage Trust

FLITTING, A RITE OF SPRING
1911—1934

It's hard not to become distracted when reading old newspapers at the History Center. Those pages bring to mind all sorts of information and raise all kinds of questions. Patterns emerge as well.

When looking for articles about growing things, we kept stumbling upon long lists of people smack dab in the middle of the front page—lists of people who were moving. These pieces usually appeared in the first April issue. A front-page article of the April 6th, 1911 edition of the *Republican,* subtitled, "Annual Observance of April 1st as Flitting Day," lists Dr. Snyder's move from 160 Franklin Avenue to 184 Franklin. Then like dominoes, his neighbor, Elmer Smith, left 226 Franklin to move into 160 Franklin! Meanwhile Joseph Sterck moved from Water Street to the house on E. Main vacated by J. M. Chesnutt, and Mr. Chesnutt moved into the house at 226 Franklin vacated by Elmer Smith!

People move for a variety of reasons. A change of employment, family size, or increased or decreased wealth may cause a family to move into other quarters.

But why in April? And why the term "flitting?" In 1911, about twenty families moved in spite of "muddy roads," and in 1913, even a measles epidemic didn't postpone the moves. That year, there were enough changes to "keep

217

the gas man and the telephone lineman busy for a spell."

By the thirties, when the Great Depression hit, the number of "flittings" diminished substantially. "Usually, when April 1 rolls around, anywhere from 40 to 100 families in the boro pack up their belongings and move. Maybe it's only down the street a few doors and maybe it's to the other side of town, but nevertheless they move," wrote a reporter in 1934, before he listed 14 fourteen families and concluded, "Perhaps local residents are getting more staid and settled..."

We might credit our Scots-Irish ancestors with the custom. When we see February 2 on the calendar and think of Punxsutawny Phil, those in Scotland see Candlemas, the day renters must tell their landlords whether they will renew the lease or move—"sit or flit." Then the search for new quarters and haggling over rents begins, and on the 25th of May, departing tenants must leave by noon, there is no time for cleaning, and a new family settles in.

Might our ancestors have followed the traditions of the home country, but moved the lease dates to April 1 through March 30th?

No matter the reason, the logistics of the day must have been mind-boggling. How many wagons or trucks were necessary to move 15, 25, 35 or 100 families? How many strong men? How did one family pack up, tidy the house, and a new family move in, all in one day? Our early directories list no more than six liveries or drayers in town. Every piece of rolling stock in town must have been called into use!

We did note that some families traditionally moved "into town" during the winter months, then returned to their farms when spring rolled around. In 1885 both the Gourleys and the Bloods returned to their farms. Some, too, moved into new homes where workmen had finished the interiors during the winter months. But for the most part, the families moving on "flitting day" were renters. And move they did—flitting from White to East Main, from Short Street to Taylor, and from Maple to Western. What a day must April first have been long ago!

Might trucks like this one that Dick & Miles used to deliver fruit have been used on "Flitting Day" to transport household belongings from one house to another?
Photographer Frederick E. Knapp, Brookville
Courtesy Brookville Heritage Trust

Between 1830 and 1902 the Globe Hotel, renamed the Jefferson House, occupied the northwest corner of Main Street and Diamond Alley. There were stables behind the hotel.
Photographer Frederick E. Knapp
Courtesy Brookville Heritage Trust

Built in 1902, the Jefferson Hotel before its 1910 transformation into the Columbia Theater.
Postcard JCHC

GOOGLING THE COLUMBIA
1918

Google (the search engine noun that's become a verb) "Columbia Theater" on the Internet and you will find this: "I believe that this theater was converted from a house or hotel into a movie theater. I would speculate that the builder added the inclined floor on top of the original flat floor. That would explain the 'incline' that you walk up to get to the seats."

At the History Center we look for factual information to back up that kind of hearsay, so what are the facts as gleaned from newspapers of the times, from Steve McPherson, who owns and is preserving the building, and from the building itself?

When war raged in Europe in 1917-1918 people nationwide flocked to the silent films. Brookville had no real movie theater, just opera houses and church halls, but people were acquainted with "picture plays" because several were shown in various buildings between 1907 and 1920. Then in the spring of 1918 Frank Brown, Mayburg (Forest County), purchased the New Jefferson Hotel from Philip J. Allgeier. He intended to turn it into a movie theater.

The plot west of Diamond Alley on Main Street had been occupied almost from 1830 when Brookville streets were first laid out. Various owners operated the Globe Hotel there between 1830 and 1857 when C. N. Kretz bought it and renamed it the Jefferson House. Another

221

succession of owners operated the hotel between 1864 and 1883 when Magnus Allgeier and L. L. Reitz purchased it. Later Philip Allgeier purchased the property from his father, tore it down in 1902, and then built the five-story New Jefferson Hotel. When Jefferson County went "dry" in 1916, he closed the hotel, and two years later Brown purchased it.

Ray H. Richards' crew demolished the hotel barn at the rear and began construction. Like many buildings on Main Street, it appears that the Globe/Jefferson House/New Jefferson Hotel did not extend to the alley but rather had a stable at the north end of the property, so we might deduce that the theater's slanted floor was not laid over the level floor of the hotel.

Following the war's end and before Christmas, the theater opened with weekend showings of *Tarzan the Ape Man.* Ruby Buffington accompanied the silent film on the Seeburg-Smith organ that sat between the screen and the audience. After paying 20 cents for each adult and 10 cents for each child "plus the war tax," patrons entered through the lobby of the Jefferson Hotel with its fine arched ceiling and fountain complete with castle and fish. White wicker furniture offered patrons a place to sit prior to the show's beginning.

Considered the "most modern moving picture house in Penn'a" by some, the Columbia had a tile floor entrance, exterior marquis, 500 "nice hardwood seats," and a high ceiling. The 33-foot height would accommodate a balcony where an additional 350 people could sit.

222

A curtain of special construction [the first curtain that exists today], "velvety brown carpets on the aisles," "mellow electric lights," and velvet trimmings on the white stucco walls made the Columbia a most attractive venue. So that live shows could be accommodated, a "complete set of scenery" was available, too.

Silent movies continued to be popular through the twenties. When *The Jazz Singer* premiered nationally in October of 1927, Brookville featured Wallace Beery n the silent film, *Casey at the Bat*. But by March 11th, 1929, Brookville folks could both see and hear *The Barker*.

Movie attendance grew, then when it began to wane during the Great Depression, "Bank Night" was created. People came hoping to win the random drawing that sometimes amounted to $100 and prizes like dishes, curtains, and other household items. The ushers sometimes had to turn people away, too. In 1939 when *Gone With the Wind* opened, the line stretched west on Main Street to the corner.

During World War II, movies continued to be popular, especially with young women in bobby sox whose beaus were serving abroad, but then television arrived, crowds diminished, and the Columbia eventually closed, opening and closing periodically as one exhibitor after another tried to foster a return of "going to the movies."

Finally in the spring of 1989 Bill Crain announced the purchase of the building and the

Scarlet Cord's (a nonprofit organization) plan to develop a "Christian Youth Center." Under the leadership of the Scarlet Cord board of directors, the theater is under continuing preservation and now is the site for contemporary music concerts, programs like the Laurel Pageant, and world premieres like *Derby Time*, Sue Benigni's musical play that was produced there in 2005!

So, what are the facts? Was the theater converted from a house or hotel into a movie theater? Yes and no. The front or lobby area is the hotel once known as the New Jefferson Hotel. Did the builder add the inclined floor on top of the original flat floor? No. The builder tore down the barn at the rear of the hotel and added a new auditorium with an inclined floor that followed the slope of the hillside and assured moviegoers a good view of the silver screen! And that they did for many, many years!

After Frank Brown purchased the Jefferson Hotel in 1918, he added a movie theater in the rear and a marquee and ticket booth in the front. The Columbia Grill, operated by George Christy is on the right, and Presto, probably a dry cleaning establishment, occupies space to the left.
Photographer Frederick E. Knapp
Courtesy Brookville Heritage Trust

Prior to WWI, Dr. Wayne Snyder operated a small hospital in this building on Franklin Avenue. When the Spanish influenza hit the county in 1918, the Red Cross used the facility.

A PAST PANDEMIC
1918

We don't know when or even if there will be a pandemic in our future, but the word has certainly entered our 21st century vocabulary. Each new death from avian or bird flu in another part of the world raises the question: will such an event happen during our lifetimes and will it affect us here in Jefferson County?

News articles and television programs about bird flu often include a reference to Spanish Influenza or the pandemic of 1918. Incorrectly named because it did not originate in Spain but correct because it was a virus or flu, people in Jefferson County did not escape its deadly consequences. By the time it began to subside in November 1918 one writer estimated more Americans had died of the Spanish Influenza between September 9 and November 9 than among American Expeditionary Forces in France. Prior to the flu's onset, obituaries listed weekly in Brookville newspapers numbered between one and eleven. As the flu peaked the *Jeffersonian Democrat* simply listed the names of the dead in a column—30 one week, 27 the next, then 15.

Spain was the first country to report this disease, but no one knows how or where it actually began. Ultimately it became pandemic, a worldwide epidemic, killing 21 to 40 million people including more than a half-million Americans. Fever, chills, coughs, aches, pains, as well

227

as general tiredness and weakness characterized this influenza. A victim's temperature, heart rate, and breathing rate increased. It led to pneumonia and death, particularly for the young and the old.

In the United States the flu first hit soldiers stationed at Fort Riley, Kansas, in early March of 1918 spreading to Philadelphia, Boston, Chicago, and San Francisco. Indiana County reported influenza in September and in October the *Jeffersonian Democrat* reported the first death from the virus to occur in Jefferson County. She was Viola A. Buzard, a fourteen-year-old girl who lived in Rose Township and who died on October 2. Twenty-one days later, the paper stated, "County toll is 200." Mining communities like Big Soldier, Conifer, Eleanora, Florence, Ramsaytown, Reynoldsville, Rossiter, and Wishaw were hit particularly hard. Wishaw reported 116 of its 375 residents down with the flu. When it was over sixty-five people were dead there or more than one of every eight.

Schools became hospitals. Annabelle Osborne, Brookville, was eight in 1918. When interviewed she recalled, "They died so fast, they hauled them out like flies...they didn't take time for funerals. They just dug a hole and put them in."

Medical staffs and hospitals within the county were swamped with the sick. Adrian Hospital, built in 1888 in Punxsutawney by Adrian Iselin for Adrian miners, had quickly become a general hospital. Its beds were kept full. Dr. John E. Grube had established a small hospital in Punxsutawney's business district in 1908. It too was swamped.

The new Brookville Hospital was in the planning stages, however, Dr. Wayne Snyder operated a small hospital on Franklin Avenue where Doctors Lynch and Prusakowski practiced more recently. The Red Cross opened a free hospital there and the newspaper warned, "The only sure way of receiving a visit by a physician has been to lie in wait for him at his office door." Nurses were at a premium.

"Virtually everyone who has escaped the disease or who has recovered has turned in to help where possible." Dr. Matson fell ill as did undertaker H. Brady Craig, forcing the entire staff of the Reitz Furniture Company to devote its time to handling funerals.

Almost as soon as the epidemic was recognized in Pennsylvania, communities were ordered to close down places where people gathered, like theaters, saloons, schools, churches, and public meeting houses. This was done in Brookville and supplies were needed in Europe, the Red Cross storeroom closed.

The pandemic ceased to exist officially in November of 1918 but local papers reported cases into the next year. Philadelphia was the American city with the highest death toll, and October turned out to be the deadliest month— 195,000 Americans dead.

Recently scientists examined the lung tissue of a victim of the 1918 influenza pandemic. The genetic coding sequence bears a strong similarity to the coding sequence found in the current bird flu virus

Is a preventative or cure waiting to be discovered? Probably. But until then communities have been advised to have an emergency plan in reserve. It makes sense, too, for individuals to follow the warnings for airborne disease prevention. If you develop coughs and sneezes, don't mingle, cover your nose and mouth, and wash your hands often.

HAIL TO THE CHIEF!
1918—2008

Yes indeed, it was a big day when former president Bill Clinton rode into Brookville, drove up the hill to "Knowledge Knob" (that's what the hill where the old Central School once stood was called a century ago), and stood on the porch at 300 Barnett Street to campaign for his wife Hillary. But contrary to what some folks thought, his visit was not the first time a former president had come to town!

Among the documents housed in the History Center archives are the programs of annual teachers' institutes that began in 1856 and continued for more than a century. Most of the teachers in schools large and small throughout Jefferson County would come to Brookville, stay in one of the many hotels on Main Street or in private homes, and attend lectures and performances. These institutes were intended to improve the skills of the young women and men who had begun teaching when they were barely older than some of their students and to inspire and entertain them, too.

In 1918, with the ink barely dry on the armistice ending World War I, most of the 353 teachers in the county gathered in the newly-opened Columbia Theater and listened over several days to speeches and lectures delivered by education experts. They watched an illustrated lecture presented by a Colonel Havers and heard the Adelphi Concert Artists. Then on the last

231

evening of the institute, they moved to the Methodist Church where an audience of 1300 welcomed former President William Howard Taft.

The 27th president of the United States had served as secretary of war under President Theodore Roosevelt and had his support for the presidency. He took office in 1908, then broke with Roosevelt prior to the election of 1912, and ran as a Republican in opposition to Roosevelt who ran as a Progressive and Wilson who ran as a Democrat. Wilson won.

With Wilson in the White House, Taft moved on to Yale Law School and the presidency of the American Bar Association. He opposed prohibition and advocated for world peace. During the war he was co-chair of the National War Labor Board and helped set national labor policy that reduced strikes and generated union support for the war.

Taft came to Brookville by train and stayed in the home of Mr. and Mrs. S. S. Henderson, where Altman & Montgomery are located today. The local editor wrote, "For the first time in its history Brookville has been honored with the presence of a former President of the United States." Taft spoke on *The Great War* and elaborated on Wilson's proposed League of Nations for about ninety minutes.

The next day at noon, a select group of gentlemen who had named themselves the "Three-fifty Club" gathered in a local banquet hall to have dinner with the president. Prior to Taft's visit they had decided to keep the event small, and in order to limit the diners, the expense for each would increase. The fee of $3.50 was assessed, the equivalent of nearly $50 today. They had decked themselves out in top hats, white vests and ties, and their best suits.

Nothing was amiss. "But, lo! And behold!" wrote the editor, "The seat of honor at the head of the table was vacant!" President Taft had been spirited away to the teachers' institute in Clarion!

Four years later, Calvin Coolidge, who was not yet president, was the featured speaker, but this time the institute met in Reynoldsville at the First Methodist Church. He'd been the running mate of Warren G. Harding in 1920, and would be elected in 1924. According to the local editor, "Silent Cal" presented "one of the most scholarly addresses."

Vice-presidents and presidential candidates have visited Brookville, too. Prior to World War I, Vice-President Thomas R. Marshall of Indiana came to town to visit his friend, Benjamin Shively (D) who represented that state in the U. S. Senate. Shively was married to Emma Jenks, the daughter of the Honorable George A. Jenks (D), who had served in the U. S. Congress and as both solicitor general of the United States and Assistant Secretary of the Interior. The Shively's summered in the large Victorian home south of Buff's Ice Cream parlor.

Perennial presidential candidate Harold Stassen visited Brookville during his first campaign in 1948, and JCHS board member Jon

Noonan was in the crowd. Finally, local candidate, Charles Glenn of Corsica, campaigned in town, too, when he was an Independent candidate for the presidency in 1948. The History Center has posters to prove it!

Campaigning for his wife in 2008, former president Bill Clinton visited Brookville.

Photographer Wrayanne Clapie

WHEN THE PRIDE OF THE WOODS BLOOMS IN JUNE

1936

"In many places the larger streams flow through deep and narrow valleys, bordered by high and precipitous hills, the combination of which furnishes many of the elements of the beautiful in natural scenery." These are the words historian Ament Blose used in 1876 to describe Jefferson County.

A little more than a decade later, historian Kate M. Scott added to the description by listing the flowers that could be seen in such abundance—"the sweet trailing arbutus, so much quoted in song and story...the viola, anemones, cerulia, May-flowers, field daisies, ox-eye daisies, lady slipper, wild columbine, the brilliant mountain pink, wake robin, wild roses, eglantines, hawthorn, dogwood." And finally, "In the fields are found magnificent lilies, while the pride of the woods is the brilliant laurel and the lovely rhododendron, which in season are nowhere found in greater profusion or more rich in coloring."

Scott was right. Mountain laurel and its near relative, the rhododendron, are nowhere found in greater profusion than in the eastern half of the United States. From the Florida panhandle west to Louisiana, north through Indiana and southern Quebec, and from north to south in the Appalachian Mountains, its pink, white, and rose blossoms fill the understories of countless hardwood forests in great profusion during May, June, or early July.

Descriptions in local newspapers of walks and picnics among the trees and group photographs taken in the woods are evidence that people living here have long enjoyed the natural beauty of the mountain laurel. However, no celebration of its beauty occurred until the harsh realities of the Great Depression hung like a cloud over the country in the 1930s.

Less than a half-century after Scott had described its natural beauty, life in Jefferson County had turned from promising to bleak. It was then that local folks came up with the idea to host a festival celebrating the beauty of the laurel. It would provide some fun during the dark days, and perhaps bring visitors into the area with money to spend.

The first Western Pennsylvania Laurel Festival took place during July 1936 in Brookville. Governor James H. Earle crowned Ethel Ellenberger of Punxsutawney as the first Laurel Queen. Newspaper articles recommended two routes to view the laurel, and entertainment included an air show and a "lady chute jumper."

The originators intended the event to move to different locations around the county each year so as to spread the anticipated economic benefits. Punxsutawney hosted subsequent festivals in 1937 and 1938, and then the darkening clouds of war intervened. After three successful festivals, one in Brookville and two in Punxsutawney, the Western Pennsylvania Laurel

Festival ceased, although the automobile club continued to promote tours of the laurel fields. Finally in1959 the Laurel Festival was reborn as an annual Brookville event.

The United Natural Gas Company had made it a practice to invite people to tour the Sigel field during the laurel season to see the colorful displays. Early in 1959 members of the Brookville Chamber of Commerce met with officials UNG officials to talk about establishing an annual laurel festival.

That year in June Joyce Robb was crowned the new laurel queen. A carnival, sidewalk sales, street dancing, and a parade drew crowds to the downtown area, while other festival goers drove to the Laurel Fields between Sigel and Clear Creek State Park. Since that time the Western Pennsylvania Laurel Festival has been an annual event in Brookville.

Like the Groundhog Festival, an occasion celebrated in nearly twenty other communities nationwide as well as in Punxsutawney, other communities host laurel festivals, too. One that is well known happens each year in Wellsboro, Tioga County, home of the Pennsylvania Grand Canyon. Begun in 1938, this festival occurs the second weekend of June. Some celebrations of Pennsylvania's official state flower are paired with music like the Mountain Laurel Celtic Festival in Bushkill and the Mountain Laurel Autoharp Concert Series in Newport. The states of Kentucky and Georgia host mountain laurel festivals. Begun in 1931, Kentucky claims to host the "oldest continuous laurel festival in the world." And like the Western Pennsylvania Laurel Festival of Jefferson County, it too traces its roots to the Great Depression years.

In May, June, and July, the forests of Jefferson County are filled with the soft pink and mauve blooms of the state flower, the mountain laurel, and its close relative, the rhododendron, shown here.
Photographer Frederick E. Knapp, Brookville
Courtesy BrookvilleHeritage Trust

THEIR HIGHNESSES, THE LAUREL QUEENS
1936–2007

In 2007 the fiftieth young woman to wear the queen's tiara was crowned during the Western Pennsylvania Laurel Festival. Begun in 1936 to promote the area's great natural beauty and greater appreciation of this wonderful asset, the festival ceased during World War II, then resumed again in 1959.

To celebrate the occasion the History Center contacted more than half of the former queens and asked them about their lives today and their memories of their reigns. We discovered their lives typify the lives of women during the last five decades. They are mothers and grandmothers, single, newly married, and divorced. Some live nearby, others traveled far. Some are students, some work, some don't; but even if it rained on their parade, all have good memories of their experience.

Mekka Dusch Spence (2006) is newly married to a military man and wrote from Colorado that she enjoys "running the house" while awaiting his deployment to Iraq. "I learned a lot being Laurel Queen—staying down to earth, being myself, and not letting the crown go to my head!"

Catherine Flannigan Zerba (1963), on the other hand, is the mother of three boys, grandmother of six, and all live in the Seneca area. She was Miss Clarion State College before enter-

239

ing the WPLF competition where she played the piano and won. "I was crowned by the governor of Pennsylvania! I met so many people. Then I went on to the Miss Pennsylvania competition."

Another former queen who'd entered a previous competition was Judi Bell Reitz (1972), Summerville. She choreographed and performed a dance routine to *Raindrops Keep Falling On My Head* for the Miss Teenage Brookville competition in 1970. Then people encouraged her to enter the WPLF contest. "Had I picked a theme at that time, it would have been to make people smile and feel happy....I will never forget the memory of the beautiful smiles from the guests of Jefferson Manor. Since it was a long parade, it was very easy for me to get off the back of Alex Deemer's antique car, and take time to walk over and greet them....I wanted to make them feel very special and welcome, but they made me feel special." Today she has remarried and lives in Brookville.

Karla Yates Dillon (1989) is a former queen who moved away. Her brother saw her perform in the Brookville production of *Babes in Toyland* and urged her to compete. "If he hadn't suggested it, I doubt I ever would have done it." Mary Ann Manfroni coached the opening dance number. "This part of the pageant wasn't judged, but since I had no dancing lessons (or ability)—it was probably more nerve-wracking for me than anything else!" An interview, talent competition, evening gown competition, and questions followed. "My application stated that I like to cook—and Bill Rehkopf from Magic 96 asked me

240

about my favorite thing to make. My reply was macaroni and cheese! To this day, my family still laughs about that!" In 1995 Karla married her dance partner from the pageant and moved to New Hampshire where they live today with their two children.

Caron Walter Heigel (2001), Sigel, graduated from Brookville Area High School, majored in psychology at Slippery Rock University, and earned a doctorate. She too lacked dance experience. "I remember having to practice the dance at home in order to make sure I was getting everything right—I had no dance experience. I had been playing the piano since I was ten years old and chose to play a piece. That required lots of practice and more focused lessons than I had previously had. We also had an evening gown segment where we had to walk back and forth on the stage as our bios were read. I remember being concerned about that part because I could see myself falling flat on my face! And you had to remember to smile at all times...I don't know how many times the pageant organizers told us that."

Like others, too, it did rain on Caron's parade! "The day of the parade was the only rainy day that week—all the other days were gorgeous. We were supposed to be in convertibles, but due to the rain the tops were up, which was disappointing. Additionally, we were supposed to sing the National Anthem for the old timer's baseball game, but it was rained out."

Nevertheless, despite the rain, like other former WPLF queens, Caron's memories are good. "This was a way for me to feel active in my community and hopefully I was able to give back to my community."

Governor Earle of Pennsylvania was on hand in 1936 to crown Ethel Ellenberger as the first Western Pennsylvania Laurel Festival Queen.
Photographer Frederick E. Knapp
Courtesy Brookville Heritage Trust

BROOKVILLE'S "POSTER CHILD" AND THE MYSTERY OF THE MISSING CORNERSTONE

1939

Sometimes an organization features a work of art on its annual poster. Or a smiling child with crutches. Or a river! Pennsylvania's Department of Conservation and Natural Resources 2005 poster featured the West Branch of the Susquehanna as the "River of the Year."

In 2001 the National Trust for Historic Preservation (NTHP) chose Brookville's Northside School Building as its "poster child." Completed in 1939 as a Public Works Administration (PWA) project of the Roosevelt administration, the school district preserved and updated the building several years ago, and it has been home to kindergarteners and their teachers ever since.

One fall during Passport to the Past, our program for elementary students, we visited the Northside building. An activity at the History Center helped us identify architectural styles, and, as they sketched the Northside building, they took note of the paned windows and pediments typical of colonial architecture.

They sketched the building from the front. Then we decided to look at it from all angles and hunt for the cornerstone—that special stone laid with great ceremony when construction of a large and important building begins. We checked the east wall—no cornerstone! We checked the

243

north wall—no cornerstone! We checked the west wall—no cornerstone! Now we had a mystery—why is there no cornerstone on the Northside Elementary School building?

Brookville was in the throes of the Great Depression when school directors found the congested conditions in several school buildings to be "troublesome." By 1938 conditions warranted serious discussion and plans to fund and build a new building rapidly moved ahead. In September voters supported an increase in the bonded indebtedness, and by November the board's application for a federal PWA project grant for 45% of the total cost had been approved.

The *Brookville Republican* commented, "Work on the new project was officially instituted last Saturday [December 24, 1938] with an impromptu but impressive ceremony, with President Ralph Mayes leaning on the shovel and Secretary Kelly leaning on the pick. Dave Reid was present as straw boss, coach, referee, or time-keeper, we forget which, but after much grunting and straining and consultation of the statutes and PWA rules made and provided for such occasions, Ralph and Bill finally managed to get a little shovel full of dirt from the reluctant bosom of Mother Earth and the big project was on." But no mention is made of a cornerstone!

The project dragged through the winter due to problems with the state over a permit to bring a big shovel over the highways from Johnstown and debate between the school board and architects about which company could provide the correct color of brick. The school board prevailed and Hanley Brick in Summerville got the contract. Twenty-five men completed the foundation by April. Next came pouring the concrete floor slabs and laying brick. By the fall of 1939, the walls were up but the building wasn't ready for occupancy. That happened right before Christmas vacation. During this time, there is no mention of laying a cornerstone. Today the building has no signage identifying it as the Northside Elementary School built in 1939!

The debate between preserving a structure and building anew, particularly when it comes to schools and other buildings that require adherence to building and safety codes is neverending. There was debate when the school board made the decision to preserve and adapt the Northside building. Would it be worth the expense? Preservationists, including the NTHP, certainly think it was.

Just like the mother who knows she cannot save every drawing her kindergartener brings home, we know we cannot preserve all buildings that exist. But we can preserve and protect a portion of them. We are fortunate that the Punxsutawney Area Historical & Genealogical Society preserved a one-room country school, and that the Brookville Area School District preserved and adapted Northside. And we are fortunate that an organization like Preservation Pennsylvania keeps us posted about structures important to our past. Since 1993 three school buildings in Jefferson County have made their at-risk list: Falls Creek Elementary; the Jefferson Street School in Punxsutawney; and Big Run Elementary School. What will become of these three? No one knows?

Jean Cutler, director of the Bureau for Historic Preservation, says, "Schools are a kind of building that are near and dear to people's hearts. There's this association of growing up in a community with a school and people value that experience. They were iconic to their lives and played an important role in their lives."

Schools are important. In future years students should remember that the building that sits on "Knowledge Knob" was built as the Northside Elementary School in 1939 and that it has significance to those who live here.

No cornerstone identifies the building that contractors completed in late 1939. The National Trust for Historic Preservation "Poster Child" in 2001, the building has been adapted to the educational needs of twenty-first century students.

JCHS Collections

LITTLE LEAGUE BASEBALL
IN BROOKVILLE
1950—2008

Spalding's *Baseball Guides* are a wealth of information about the game that began in earnest in our country after the Civil War. Beginning with the National Association (1871-1875) seven leagues have played professionally in this country. Some like the Union League (1884), Players League (1890) and the Federal League (1914-1915) had brief seasons. The American Association played between 1882 and 1891. Today's leagues are both more than a century old, with the National League beginning in 1876 and the American League in 1901.

According to western Pennsylvania historian Robert Van Atta, early baseball also included professional minor league, regional semi-pro, industrial, railroad, mining, and sandlot leagues. For example, *Spalding's* refers to three in Pennsylvania. Akron, E. Liverpool, Canton, Sharon, Youngstown, Newcastle, McKeesport, and Erie made up the Ohio and Pennsylvania League (1905-1912.) To the South, Uniontown, Clarksburg, Charleroi, Connellsville, Fairmont, and Grafton played as the Pennsylvania-West Virginia League (1908-1909.) And to the east Williamsport, Harrisburg, Lancaster, Reading, Johnstown, Trenton, Altoona, and Wilmington played as the Tri-State League (1904-1914.)

On a more local level the 1877 diary of Cyrus Blood refers to highly competitive games between the young men of Brookville and Reynoldsville. But while he religiously records the scores of the newly formed National League and of various college games, he gives no indication of any sort of local "league" structure during that year.

An early photograph in the History Center's collection shows the 1891 Brookville team. These young men wore collared shirts with "Brookville" lettered across the front and dark pants that reached their ankles. Striped caps and belts completed the uniform. The two bats in the picture are narrower than present-day bats and the catcher did have a mask.

Locally there were at least two efforts to involve boys of a younger age in organized team play. The Brookville Juniors organized in 1904. A newspaper snippet mentioned "Earl Fuller was organizer and manager of the team which played one season. Money to purchase uniforms for the team was obtained by public subscription to outfit the boys who ranged in age from 16 to 18 years." They played DuBois, Punxsy, Hawthorn, Reynoldsville, and Brockwayville during that one season and had no losses!

H. C. "Dutch" Endress managed another younger team. One player was John Shively. His father, Benjamin, was a U. S. Senator from the state of Indiana and had married Emma Jenks of Brookville. The family summered here in the big Victorian house above what is now Buff's Ice Cream. During his summers, John played ball and even named the team. The "North Stars" played 13 games against teams from Reyn-

248

oldsville, DuBois, Brockway, and New Bethlehem. The boys wore collared shirts and knickers with dark sox, but caps and shoes seemed to vary from boy to boy.

Later when Shively was a student at Yale he had a small workroom in Brookville where he developed an electric refrigerator. He called his company the North Star Refrigerator Company!

Finally, in 1939 Williamsport gave birth to Little League Baseball. Teams of boys between the ages 5 to 12 played on a reduced-size field. Their goal—to play in the "World Series" in Williamsport!

Little League baseball first appeared in Brookville in 1950. Tom White described the field at the Memorial Park as "a beautiful ballpark...encircled by a green, wooden fence. Behind centerfield was a manually operated scoreboard where inning-by-inning totals were posted. The scoreboard had lights, which let the players, managers, the crowd, and yes, even the umpires, know the ball-strike count and the number of outs. The lights were operated by the official scorekeeper who sat in the press box behind home plate."

Tom also reminded his readers of the dugouts that filled with water after a sudden rainstorm!

Local businesses, Brookville Creamery, Fulton Chevrolet, Sterck's, and Riverside Market, supported the first teams to play in 1950.

The passage of Title IX in 1972 led to a Little League rule change the next year that allowed girls to play in 1974. Did Brookville girls try out that year? If so, the History Center's not been able to document it!

Today both boys and girls try out for many divisions and play the all-American sport. Tee Ball is for ages 5 to 8. Minors are ages 7 to 11. Little League or the Majors are ages 9 to 12. Juniors are ages 13 to 14. Both baseball and softball are available for older persons and there is also a division for children with disabilities.

What was once a pick-up game on a sandlot has become a well-organized activity for young people in communities throughout all fifty states and more than eighty countries. Each year more than 20,000 teams worldwide are hearing the call "Play Ball!"

Sterks, like many local businesses, sponsored a Little League team in 1955.

McMurray Collection

BROOKVILLE SAYS MERRY CHRISTMAS!

1985

For more than twenty years, Brookville folks and visitors have enjoyed the entertainment, fun, food, and festivity of a Victorian Christmas Celebration. The town hosted its first one just three years after the formation of Historic Brookville, Inc., the organization that recognizes the significant late 19th century architecture of Main Street as well as its potential for economic benefit for the community.

Programs, tabloids, and brochures from the History Center's archives trace the event's evolution. For instance, the four-column program for the first one in 1985 listed events that have been repeated nearly every year since: caroling, strolling brass ensembles, Christmas Tree Lane, Living Windows, craft fair, Santa Claus, buggy rides, dancing in one form or another, food, and, of course, the Live Nativity!

Some activities have come and gone. In 1977, Brookville Community Theater, under the direction of Dorrie Altman, entertained the community with a large-scale production of *Babes in Toyland*. Between 1990 and 1999, the Jefferson County Historical Society sponsored gingerbread house contests. In 1997, the Pittsburgh Gibson Girls offered programs on the dress, furnishings, and social practices of those long-ago days. For several years, Civic Club lined Jefferson and Pickering streets with hundreds of luminaries. Mystery dinner theater parties were once popular, too.

The annual celebration involves organizations, individuals, and businesses that willingly create this magical introduction to the holiday season. The Brookville Borough Arts Council, through grants and contributions, has arranged for wonderful entertainment through the years like the River City Brass Band, Dear Friends, the Pittsburgh Oratorio Society, the Nutcracker ballet, and the Cashour Marionettes. People flock to performances of local groups like the Clarion Dulcimers, Fieldstone and Friends, and rock musicians, too.

Visits of famous personages like Washington, Franklin, Dickens, and Lincoln have been well-received. A re-enactor like Jim Getty at Gettysburg can be so realistic that young and old alike almost believe they've met the president!

Those printed programs document when new events began. Randy Bartley produced the first walking tour in 1991 and these continue to this day, as do the "Ghosts, Myths, & Legends," candlelight tours. Between 1995 and 2003, the Jefferson County Historical Society and Brookville Community Theater collaborated on walked tours based on local events. *Six Days* told the stories of the Henderson brothers and the Civil War. *To Make the Devil Wonder* brought to life the people connected with the exhumation of a black body.

Just as tea parties became popular during the Victorian Age, so have they have become popular here. The children's tea party began in 1996 with parlor games, music, music, stories, and refreshments. Now there are three—for ladies, school-age boys and girls, and one for preschool children and their mothers.

Several other events provide fun and a trip back in time for adults and children alike. Grace Lutheran Church's congregation invited the community to experience a typical 19th century worship service in 1995, and later turned it into an annual church social with poetry reading, music, and much frivolity in the cozy surroundings of Brookville's oldest church building.

Just as that church sanctuary carries a person back in time, so do the ballrooms hidden high in many of Brookville's larger structures. Dancing was an important part of 19th and early 20th century life here, so it was only natural that the Victorian Christmas Celebration include a dance! The first in 1992 took place at the Pine Crest Country Club, a fine place for dancing, but not exactly Victorian! In 1996, thanks to the efforts of Richard and Beverly Smaby and the cooperation of Dr. Mark McKinley, McCracken Hall (the third floor of Landmark Square) became the site for the ball, a true re-creation of the balls once held there.

When Brookville's Historic District and its many century-old buildings become populated with costumed clerks, young people, and old ones, too, the ambiance of life more than a hundred years ago is created. Some might question why the effort put forth by so many individuals, organizations, and business matters? Why prepare soup and sandwiches in the church kitchen? Why dress up? Why shiver in front of the Living Windows?

In today's world of high tech and instant communication, it is easy to connect with others worldwide. On the other hand, we no longer sit on our porches and chat following supper. Simple "neighboring" is less common. Celebrations like Brookville's Victorian Christmas offer us a tie to truly be neighbors, as well as a time to connect with our past. Merry Christmas, Brookville!

House tours introduced in 1993 quickly became sell-outs. The camaraderie that develops among strangers as people travel from home to home is fun. The decorations are always lovely, viewing some of Brookville's most interesting interiors is a once-a-year opportunity, and sometime "live mannequins" take a person back in time.

WHAT DO YOU DO AT A HISTORY CENTER?

2004

History Center? "What's a history center?" It is not uncommon to hear that question around Brookville. For more than three decades, people were used to hearing about the Jefferson County Historical and Genealogical Society. Some had even visited the little house on Jefferson Street where the society maintained a library and rooms filled with old stuff. School groups came for a lesson on local history. Genealogists came to look up obituaries and other family information, and people traveling I-80 would stop off and take a look at the items displayed or use the restrooms

The library and much of the old stuff are now found at 172-176 Main Street in the building that has Jefferson County History Center across the front. One show window displays logging tools and another shows beekeeping and soap-making equipment. The other two show windows look more like a typical shop, and it is through the shop door that visitors enter. Once inside, people will find the History Center Shop where books and maps about the county are available as well as a selection of gift items. There's a selection of quality toys and books for children, too.

But items for sale are not the only thing available in the History Center. Behind the shop and up a short flight of steps, are the research rooms. An assistant is available there to help genealogists, students, and those who want to find out about a particular topic. One year, besides hundreds of genealogists, our assistant helped a student from Indiana University of PA who needed documents about the Marlin Opera House for a class project and visitors from Oil City who grew up remembering the old ladder factory. She helped folks use old newspapers, surname and topical files, books, maps, directories, and indexes, and often showed them how to navigate the Internet.

The History Center is also a museum. There are galleries where the stories of Jefferson County are told through objects, documents, and photographs. In 2005, the stories of the Civil War, WWII, and the Vietnam Conflict were portrayed in the Parker Gallery on the first floor. Visitors could see the diary with the bullet hole that couldn't protect Thomas Reynolds McCullough from his death at Gettysburg. They could also see the Life Magazine article depicting Dr. Dinsmore's miraculous removal of a large live mortar from a Vietnamese soldier. Things were labeled and exhibit panels described what happened.

Upstairs in two smaller galleries, *Creative Minds at Work* showed how the arts developed in Jefferson County. People here have always tried to express themselves through art, music, drama, sculpture, and writing. Whether it was a Native American decorating a pot rim or Daniel Long embellishing the rifle he made, the creative spirit was here.

A large section of the second floor is devoted to the Bowdish Model Railroad Layout. The layout is always available for viewing. On the last Saturday of every month, the Bowdish Volunteers run the trains for visitors. The layout is redesigned each year to feature a particular theme. One year, visitors could see how people have celebrated throughout the county at events like the Laurel Festival, Groundhog Day, and the annual pancake breakfast in Sykesville.

The History Center is located in the Nathan Greene Edelblute Building built in the 1840s and 1875. The parlor walls remain as they were in 1890 when Adda Edelblute married Elmer Pearsall there. Typical 19th century furnishings from the JCHS collections are there to see.

The History Center opened its doors on March 27, 2004, the bicentennial of Jefferson County. Since that time, thousands of people have visited the exhibits, attended public programs, or used the research room. Located just ½ block east of the Jefferson County Courthouse, visiting the History Center is a worthwhile way spend some time.

Check out www.jchconline.org or the Facebook page to learn more about this most interesting destination.

INDEX

Adams County, 138

Adrian Hospital, 230

Aharrah, Larry, 27

Allegheny River, 120, 158

Allgeier, Magnus, 224

Allgeier, Philip J., 223, 224

Allgeier's Meadow, 197

Altman & Montgomery, 234

American Hotel, 108, 145

American House, 69

American Legion, 179

Ames, Rose Blake, 122

Amish, 17

Anderson, Charles, 83, 85, 86

Andy Hastings Gymnasium, 198

Anthony, Susan B., 153, 155, 156

Armstrong County, 5, 66

Arthurs, Richard, 113

artists, 115, 116, 117, 171, 172, 173

automobile, 146, 174, 175

aviation, 174

Bank Night, 225

Baptist Church, 14

Baptists, 211

Barnett County, 67

Barnett, Joseph, 3, 7, 22, 65, 67, 198, 207

Barr, Thomas, 7

baseball, 62, 130, 157, 158, 159, 160, 166, 167, 168, 169, 243, 249, 251, 252

Basketball, 215, 217

Baur, Albert, 107, 109, 110

Baxter, "Brush", 121

259

Beechwoods. See
Washington Township
Vocational High School

Benigni, Sue, 226

Big Run, 68, 247

Black Americans, 24

Blair County, 112

Blood, Cyrus H.,
129, 132, 157, 249

Blood, Parker P., 129

Blose, Ament, 237

Bowdish Model
Railroad Exhibit,
179

Bowdish, Charles
Albert, 90, 116,
170, 186, 189,
191, 192, 193, 194

bracket dam, 120,
200

Brady, E. R., 137

Brandon, Thomas, 6

Briggs, Helen Darr,
129

Brockway, 65, 68, 71

Brockwayville, 137,
250

Brookville Academy,
33

Brookville Area
School District,
247

Brookville Banjo,
Mandolin, and
Guitar Society, 109

Brookville Cemetery
Association, 98

Brookville Cemetery
Company, 151

Brookville Chamber
of Commerce, 239

Brookville Creamery,
184

Brookville High
School, 161, 196,
206, 215

Brookville Hospital,
231

Brookville Raiders,
205, 208

Brookville
Republican, 159

Brookville Water
Company, 70, 71

Brookville Water
Works, 71

Brotherhood of Local Firemen and Engineers, 213

Brown, Frank, 223, 227

Bucks County, 65

Buff's Ice Cream, 235, 250

Buffington, Ruby, 224

Bureau for Historic Preservation, 247

Burkett, Kenneth, 5

Burns, Ken, 137

Buzard, Viola A., 230

Callen Run, 121

Canada, 9, 37, 81

Canning, Jimmy, 109

Canning, Thomas Scribner, 107

Carnegie Science Center, 186, 188, 191, 192

Carousel Gift Shop, 114

Carroll, Mr., 27

Casino Roller Skating Rink, 26

Central School, 35, 196, 205, 233

Chautauqua, 91, 92

Chesnutt, J. M., 219

Chester County, 65

Christian Youth Center, 226

Christmas, 224, 247

Church of Christ, 213

Civil War, 15, 22, 25, 60, 61, 87, 88, 102, 104, 108, 109, 129, 137, 138, 146, 151, 154, 157, 171, 172, 183, 249

Civilian Conservation Corps, 30

Clarington, 80, 81

Clarion, 5, 12, 67, 71, 81, 112, 113, 206, 207, 216, 217, 235

Clarion County, 5

Clarion High School, 207

Clarion Normal, 197, 206

Clarion River, 12, 67, 113, 200

Clark, Elijah Heath, 47, 77

Clark, J. G., 111

Clark, William, 111

Clarke, Ann Amelia, 95, 98

Clarke, Nell, 116, 170, 172

Clayville, 80

Clear Creek State Park, 30, 239

Clearfield County, 67

Clinton, Bill, 233

Clinton, Hillary, 233

Coal Glen, 205

Columbia Amusement Company, 126

Columbia Theater, 212, 222, 223, 224, 225, 227, 233

Columbus, 37

Conway, James, 27

Cook Forest State Park, 30

Cook, Anthony Wayne, 30

Cook, John, 30

Cooksburg, 30

Coolidge, Calvin, 235

Coon, William, 80, 81

Corbet, Charles, 47, 77, 156

Corsica, 137, 216, 236

cradle, grain, 19

Craig, Hugh Brady, 231

Craig, Margaret, 115, 116

Craig, Samuel A., 138, 139

Crain, Bill, 225

Cummins, 131

Daedalus, 15

dancing, 178, 179, 180, 212, 213, 239

Darling, Paul, 139

Darr, Hope, 156

262

Darr, Maud, 160

Darr, William Thompson, 47, 77, 132

Deemer, Frank Clifton, 161

Dennison, Heidi Ulrich, 77

Department of Highways, 27

Diamond Alley, 222, 223

Dick, Mary Geist, 174, 176, 202

Dick, Walter, 31, 202

Dickey, Ada, 157, 160

Donation Lands, 65

Dr. Walter Dick Memorial Park, 31, 200, 203

DuBois Courier, 114

DuBois High School, 207

Earle, James H., 238

Edelblute, Ada, 114, 179, 259

Edelblute, Nathan Greene, 33, 99, 100, 101, 102, 111, 113

Edgewood Park Roller Rink, 212

Eldred Township, 23, 125

Eleanora, 205, 230

Elk County, 67

Ellenberger, Ethel, 238

Endres, Cleveland, 156

Endress, H. C. "Dutch", 250

Europeans, 5

Evans, Jared B., 69

Falls Creek, 68, 247

farmer, 19, 20

farming, 17, 19

First Assembly of God, 211

Fishbasket, 5

flail, 19

flitting, 219, 221

Florence, 230

Florida, 27, 237

flu, 229, 230

263

Fogle, Christopher, 80

Foradora, John H., 47, 77

Forest County, 45, 46, 67, 80, 104, 129, 131, 223

Fort Stanwix, 65

fountain, 95, 97, 98

Fourth of July, 211

Fowler, Thaddeus Mortimer, 171

Frank, David, 112

Frank, Rosetta, 100, 112

Franklin House, 83, 85

fugitive slaves, 24, 85

Fuller, Earl, 250

Fuller, Ira C., 91

Fulton Chevrolet, 202, 251

Galbraith, Principal, 34

Gateway Bowling Center, 212

George W. Heber Historical Society of Jefferson County, 151

Gettysburg, 138, 139, 140

Glenn, Charles, 236

Globe Hotel, 112, 222, 223

Gold Eagle, 213

Gordon, Isaac G., 76

Grand Army of the Republic, 137

Grant, U.S., 25

Gray, William Henry, 138, 139

Great Depression, 9, 61, 179, 220, 225, 238, 240, 246

Groundhog Festival, 239

Grube, John E., 230

Guth's Jewelry, 114

Hanley Brick, 246

Harding, Warren G., 235

Hastings, Charles Elliott "Andy", 198

Hawk, Vaughn, 196

Hays Lot, 30

Heath Township, 27, 67

Heath, Elijah, 24, 79, 85, 86

Heathville, 81

Heber, George Washington, 149, 150, 152

Heckman, Clarence, 184

Heidrick, Levi, 105

Henderson, John Wilson, 60

Henderson, S. S., 234

Henry, David, 69

Henry, William L., 47, 77

Hickory Grove Elementary School, 31, 199

Historic Brookville, Inc, 31

Horner, Dorothy, 184

Hunt, Captain, 3

I-80, 196

Ice Cream Saloon, 157

Illustrated London News, 38

Indiana, 66, 81

Indiana Normal, 206, 207

Iselin, Adrian, 230

Jackson, Lena Frank, 113

Jefferson County, 5, 6, 13, 15, 17, 19, 27, 29, 30, 37, 38, 65, 66, 67, 68, 79, 119, 120, 121, 122, 137, 138, 139, 156, 214, 215, 216, 224, 229, 230, 233, 237, 238, 240, 247

Jefferson County Bar Association, 45, 77

Jefferson County Courthouse, 68, 69

Jefferson County History Center, 12, 13, 38, 111, 112, 113, 155, 156, 179, 183, 208, 212, 219, 223,

265

233, 236, 245, 250, 251

Jefferson Hotel, 26

Jefferson House, 222, 223, 224

Jefferson Manor, 29

Jeffersonian Democrat, 72, 216, 229, 230

Jenks County, 67

Jenks, Emma, 235, 250

Jenks, George A., 235

Jenks, William P., 46, 76

Jenks, William Parsons, 45

Kelso, J.C., 139

Kennedy, "Neighbor", 34, 36, 87

Kline, Benjamin, 120

Knapp, Frederick E., 16, 28, 98, 122, 140, 145, 156, 181, 190, 215, 221, 240

Knapp, Moses, 7, 22, 67, 103, 146

Knowledge Knob, 233

Kretz, Charles N., 108, 223

Lake Erie, 65, 81

Laurel Queen, 241

Leathers garage, 179

Lee, 130

Lewis, Jason, 173

Lexington, Virginia, 130

Lincoln, Abraham, 133, 140

Litch dam, 71

Litch Mansion, 178

Litch, Thomas K., 119, 170

Little League Baseball, 251

Little Sandy, 16

Little Toby Creek, 200

Little Wonder, 121

log construction, 5

Long, Jesse C., 47, 77

Longview Hotel, 109

Longview School, 35

Lycoming County, 66

Margiotti, Charles, 74, 77

Marienville, 129

Marshall, Thomas R., 235

Massachusetts, 120, 182, 215

Matson and Heidrick, 30

Matson, Dr. Charles, 231

Matson, Richard McConnell, 27, 90, 104

Matson, Uriah, 103, 105, 106, 139

Matson's Hall, 213

Mayes, Ralph, 246

McCalmont, Alexander, 66

McCracken Hall, 178, 180

McCracken, John, 172

McCreight, Elizabeth Marlin, 156

McCreight, Martha, 33, 34, 35, 36

McCullough, Thomas Reynolds, 133, 136

McCullough, William, 14

McKean County, 67

McKnight, William J., 6, 9, 11, 17, 21, 22, 23, 46, 47, 69, 79, 80, 81, 83, 84, 87, 88, 89, 94, 95, 96, 125, 138, 147

McMurray, H. E., 147

McMurray, John, 207

McNeil, A. Ray, 166, 167, 168, 169

McPherson, Steve, 223

Means, George, 131

Melchoir, Amelia F., 60

Methodist Church, 234, 235

Methodist Episcopalians, 211

Methodists, 80

Mill Creek, 7

Miller, Silas, 121

milliners, 59, 60, 62

Miniature Railroad & Village, 186, 191, 192

Mississippi River, 119

Mitchell, John, 66

Mohawks, 4

Monongahelas, 2, 4

Moore, Charles, 33

Morris, Robert Means, 47, 77

mountain laurel, 237

Municipal Water Authority, 72

Munsey, 3

National Weather Service, 25

National Woman's Suffrage Association, 154

Native Americans, 1, 2, 3, 5

natural gas, 161, 162, 163, 164

Negroes, 80

New Jefferson Hotel, 223, 224, 226

New Year's, 211, 212, 213, 214

Newbold, Charles, 18

Nicholson Hall, 155

Noonan, Jon, 236

North Fork, 7, 15, 30, 67, 70, 71, 96, 103, 105, 120, 122, 150, 200, 201, 203

North Fork Watershed Association, 31

North Star Refrigerator Company, 251

North Stars, 250

Northside Elementary School, 35, 180, 245, 248

Northside Park, 196

Northumberland County, 65

Ohio River, 119, 249

Orr, Robert, 66

Osborne, Annabelle, 230

pandemic, 229, 231

Pantall Hotel, 110

Patterson's Drug Store, 114

Paul Darling Memorial Hall, 196, 197

Peacock, David, 18

Pearsall Hall, 26

Pearsall, Arad, 79, 80

Pearsall, Elmer, 101, 114, 179

Pel's Shoe Store, 114

Penn State University, 25

Pennsylvania Memorial Home, 87

Pennsylvania State Historical Marker, 81, 86

penny dreadfuls, 183

Perdix, 15

Perry Township, 23

Philadelphia, 230, 231

photographers, 116, 117, 147, 171, 172

Pickering Street., 28

Pinecreek Township, 21, 133, 146

Pinecrest Country Club, 180

Pittsburgh, 26, 119, 121, 205

Pittsburgh Pirates, 157

plow, 17, 18

plow, moldboard, 18

Port Barnett, 3, 21, 26, 67

Porter Township, 200

Public Works Administration, 245

Punxsutawney, 68, 80, 114, 137, 206, 216, 230, 238, 239, 247

Punxsutawny Phil, 220

Quakers, 80

Queen Victoria, 37

rafting, 26, 119

Ramsaytown, 230

269

Rebecca M. Arthurs Library, 170

Red Bank, 113

Red Bank Creek, 16, 120, 197, 202

Red Bank Navigation Company, 120, 170

Red Bank Stock Barns, 113

Red Cross, 231

Redick, O. C., 139

Redpath Lyceum Bureau, 154

Reed, John W., 47, 77

Reid, Dave, 246

Reitz Furniture Company, 231

Reitz, L. L., 224

Reynoldsville, 26, 68, 137, 158, 159, 180, 230, 235, 249, 250

rhododendron, 237, 240

Richards, Ray H., 224

Riverside Market, 213, 251

Robb, Joyce, 239

Rodgers, William, 111

Rogers, Katherine, 45

Roll, Stephen, 26

Roosevelt, Theodore, 197

Rose Township, 23, 103, 131

Rossiter, 230

Rubin's, 184

Sandt, Elizabeth Anne, 183

Sandt, Lewis Earle, 174

Sandt's drugstore, 184

Sandy Lick Creek, 15, 66, 120

Sayer, Fred, 156

Scarlet Cord, 26, 112, 226

Scots-Irish, 6

Scott, Kate M., 3, 16, 21, 23, 26, 35, 45,

77, 87, 93, 109, 117, 137, 139, 147, 171, 237, 238

Scribner, Samuel Alexander, 125

Senecas, 3, 4

shanty, 9, 10, 80

Shively, Benjamin, 235, 250

Shively, John, 250

Shofestahl, Mrs., 26

Shultz, August, 26

slaves, 23, 108

Sloane, Eric, 14

Smith, Dan, 184

Smith, Elmer, 219

Smith, Sharon, 78

Snyder, Edwin, 47, 77

Snyder, Wayne, 219, 231

Sons of Veterans Band, 26

Southerland, Charles, 23

Sowers, Dora, 59

Spanish Influenza, 229

Sprankle Mills, 30, 137

St. Clair-Jelly Orchestra, 26

Stanton, Elizabeth Cady, 153

Stassen, Harold, 235

Steadman, James, 80

Sterck, Joseph, 219

Sterck's, 251

suffrage, 153, 155

Summerville, 68, 81, 246

Sunshine Boys, 180

Susquehanna, 13, 66, 245

swimming, 31, 199, 200, 201, 202, 203

Sykesville, 68

Taft, William Howard, 234

telegraph, 25, 121

telephone, 220

Three-fifty Club, 234

timber, 16, 27, 29, 30, 119, 120, 122

Timblin, 65, 68

Tionesta, 27

Tionesta County, 67

Title IX, 217, 251

Trautman Drugs, 114

Troy, 80, 81

Truman, Alfred, 70, 89, 91, 121, 188

Underground Railroad, 79, 80, 81

United Natural Gas Company, 162, 163, 239

Valentine's Day, 182, 184

Van Atta, Robert, 249

Van Camp, Fudgeon, 21, 22, 23, 24, 26, 29, 31

Venango County, 66

Victorian Christmas Celebration, 180

Vietnam, 192

Village Improvement Association,, 95

Wallace School, 27

Washington Township Vocational School, 216

Weather, 25, 27

Wellsboro, 239

Western Auto, 114

Western Pennsylvania Laurel Festival, 180, 238, 239, 240, 241, 252

Westmoreland County, 66

White Steamer, 27

White Street Bridge, 158

Wild Cat Regiment, 139

winter, 25, 26, 27, 28, 29, 119, 178, 221

Wishaw, 230

Wood, Jethro, 18

woodworkers, 15

World War I, 65, 223, 224

World War II, 225

Worthville, 68

Wright and Pier, 121

WWI, 22, 61, 99, 130, 188

WWII, 61, 116, 241

YMCA, 26, 178, 179, 199, 203, 212, 213, 215, 216

Youmans, Elmer William, 115